A SPEEDER'S GUIDE TO AVOIDING TICKETS

"Speed enforcement in this country is a mockery. Police work has evolved to the point where the cops and everyone else in the system prefer that you speed. It makes their job easier."

"I am not writing this to encourage you to speed. You are doing that already and we both know it. In this country, 'We, the People' are supposed to be the government and 'We, the People' choose to drive cars faster than our elected officials choose to permit."

"There are some laws that can't be broken. They are the laws of physics. There is no excuse for reckless driving. The fun goes away in a hurry if 'the thrill of the chase' and poor judgment causes pain or death. Make all your trips safe ones, driven at a speed that is reasonable and prudent."

_____

JAMES M. EAGAN is a former New York State Trooper with over 20 years of experience.

A SPEEDER'S GUIDE TO AVOIDING TICKETS

SGT. JAMES M. EAGAN, N.Y.S.P. (RET.)

AVON BOOKS ◆ NEW YORK

AVON BOOKS
A division of
The Hearst Corporation
1350 Avenue of the Americas
New York, New York 10019

Copyright © 1990 by James M. Eagan
Published by arrangement with the author
Library of Congress Catalog Card Number: 91-73641
ISBN: 0-380-71733-6

First Avon Books Printing: October 1991

AVON TRADEMARK REG. U.S. PAT. OFF. AND IN OTHER COUNTRIES, MARCA REGISTRADA, HECHO EN CANADA

Printed in Canada

UNV 10

Dedicated to the memory of

TPR. ROBERT G. DUNNING
AKA: Bobby Good Guy
1941–1987

"We asked for a trooper and they sent us a song & dance man."

When everyone began to shy away from a loud mouth recruit with no street savvy, Bob would take them under his wing and teach them how to be "the man."

He taught me to use my brain to keep everyone else off balance.

He taught me the value of laughter for reducing the stress and hiding the pain.

He would understand all the real reasons for this book . . . and he would approve.

Even in his horrible death, he was my mentor. "Retire when you can. Do not fear the unknown."

As long as there are "K" troopers left who once took their Holstein 440s to the barn at quitting time. . . .

As long as bars exist in the Harlem Valley where draft beer is cheap and fights break out. . . .

As long as there are deer to hunt in the hills of Poughquag or pheasants for a good dog to work or trout to catch in the streams. . . .

Then in the evening men will in friendship gather and tip a Dewar's to your memory.

I miss you.

Acknowledgments

I would have to first thank my wife and children who, not only encouraged me but found they couldn't pass a certain door, without being dragged in to read a new portion.

Many thanks also go to Anthony & Marian Degilorma and their daughter Diane Gandino, who helped me with their prayers and constructive criticism. Marian's spelling ability also helped keep me from appearing illiterate.

Table of Contents

Preface

I suggest you plan on reading this book at least twice. The first time through should be for your entertainment and enjoyment and the second time for education. You will soon find I have pulled no punches and covered the subject in detail. There are no sacred cows or subjects that I considered too sensitive or off limits, for any reason. This book is exactly what the title indicates.

Police radio scanners were not covered in the body of this book for a number of reasons. It is felt that, only if someone is intimately aware of police operations, will the police radio scanner be of any value. In addition to them being illegal in many areas, the use of these units would also reduce the average driver's concentration that could be better spent on observing the road and listening to the C.B. radio. The number of different frequencies necessary to effectively monitor all the police radio channels would cause the driver to be subjected to constant radio chatter. This would ultimately result in his not paying attention to any transmissions.

Expect no magic formula. There is no easy checklist you can follow that will guarantee success. Rather consider your chances of getting a speeding ticket as being on a scale. The more weights you can place on your side of the fulcrum, the better are your chances of avoiding a ticket. This book is chock full of weights, both big and small. It's your decision as to which ones, and how many you choose to use.

So for most of you, what's your chances of actually avoiding a ticket after reading this book? They're a damn sight better than before you started! Enjoy.

A SPEEDER'S GUIDE TO AVOIDING TICKETS

CHAPTER 1

The Facts of Life

Why would a recently retired member of the State Police or Highway Patrol tell you how to avoid a speeding ticket when he just spent the last twenty years trying to see that you got one? For this book to have credibility I feel it would be necessary to answer that question for you before going any further. After you finish reading this short first chapter, the answer to the question "Why?" will be self-evident. In spite of the system within which I worked, I feel I made it through those two decades with my integrity still intact. (Tattered in places but still essentially intact.)

Some of my cohorts will say I am committing treason, while others, those who go to the trouble of reading the book, will say "Right On!" Sooner or later someone has to call a spade a spade and reveal the foolishness that is modern day traffic enforcement. In addition to helping you, this book is my effort in that regard.

To be quite honest, I would be perfectly happy if I were to know that you the reader would, after finishing this book, decide it wasn't worth the effort and made the decision to never exceed the posted speed limit again. I am not writing this to encourage you to speed. You are doing that already and we both know it. If you were not so inclined, there would be no reason for this book to be of interest to you. With that in mind let me now list the reasons for authoring this little bomb.

A) Hypocrisy - Speed enforcement in this country is a mockery. When I was a young recruit, I was taught the term "selective enforcement" and was told it was the act of making a special effort to nab a particular type of violator who presented a special danger. Some examples of "selective enforcement" would be a police patrol following a school bus while trying to catch anyone who was passing illegally, or running radar in a school zone. I quickly learned that the real "selective enforcement" was the freedom of nearly unlimited choice exercised by the police officer in deciding who gets a ticket and who is let off. Police work has evolved to the point where the cops and everyone else in the system prefers that you speed. It makes their job easier.

While the general public is subject to a ticket at almost any time, there are, as in every society, members of the "privileged class." In Moscow, it is my understanding that there is a special middle

2

lane for those who are not subject to the traffic laws of society.

In our country, they issue them badges and identification cards, saying they are cops. Just as the privileged class in the Soviet Union would not be inclined to travel in any lane but their special one, our privileged class often act as if they would be committing an atrosity by obeying the speed limit.

My experience has shown that if a person on an interstate is traveling in excess of thirty miles an hour OVER the speed limit, is following too close to the rear of anyone who dares impede his forward motion and almost forces other cars out of his way, there is at least a 75% chance he is a police officer. It is also very likely that he is either off duty or if working, is NOT going to an emergency. There is better than a 99% chance that, when stopped, he will not get a ticket. All cops don't speed while off duty, but those who do manage to do it with impunity.

I have heard officers rationalize the actions of their peers by making the claim that police are trained in high speed driving and so it is "not so bad." The truth is most police work in congested cities and rarely get their patrol cars up to 60 mph. The maintenance on their personal cars is also rarely as good as can be found on a highway patrol cruiser.

If everyone who was stopped had to receive a ticket, cops would also be required to obey the law and there would be no reason for you to buy this book. As long as police have the option of stopping a car and not writing a ticket, there will be abuses of the system. With rare exceptions such as a Geor-

3

gia deputy who hates all Yankees, even if they are cops, or the occasional mini-feuds that sometimes rear their ugly heads between agencies or portions of the same agency, cops would sooner face a loaded gun than ticket a ''brother'' officer. Is that so bad? I can't really say but because there are exceptions made for cops, then exceptions can be made for others such as politicians and other ''special'' people. The final result is that traffic enforcement is often exercised with prejudice and bigotry by officers who see nothing wrong with their actions.

B) More Hypocrisy - The next time you hear of a vintage car show, go look under the hood of a 1950 through 1965 American made automobile. The engine block, carburetor, wiring and other trappings are simple, basic and logical. Then go look under any car sold in the good old U.S.A. during the last five years. Our Federal Government has accomplished this metamorphosis by passing stringent pollution laws. They also succeeded in requiring every state to pass a 55 mph speed law that, only after many years, has been repealed in some areas. My point is this. If the Federal, State and Local Governments really wanted everyone to obey the speed limit, vehicles sold in this country would be legally required to have a governor that would limit the speed to 65 mph and the tampering with one would be a federal offense.

If I drove for any length of time in a marked police cruiser at 7 mph over the posted speed limit, the traffic would begin to back up behind me until some brave (or foolish) soul would dare to pass. The majority of our society does not want to be subject to the present speed laws. In this country "We, the People" are supposed to be the government and "We, the People" choose to drive cars faster than our elected officials choose to permit. Is it not logical to assume then that our elected officials, who have the capability of modifying our cars so they can't speed, know we want to go faster than the limits they have set and expect us to violate the law?

C) Still More Hypocrisy - Just two more points and I will get off this soap box. I know of no police officer or group of police officers who have ever been commended for writing less speeding tickets. Would it not seem logical that if the number of speeding arrests are reduced and the number of accidents are also reduced then either the traffic volume is down or the cops have done their job in speed enforcement? Yet my experience has shown that any time there is a reduction in the number of tickets issued, there is a knee jerk reaction to castigate the cops who are writing less tickets. Consequently, to avoid being harassed by their bosses, when people slow down, the police lower their tolerance, which is the number of miles per hour they will allow you over the speed limit, before choosing to stop you.

The only logical conclusion that can then be drawn is that the members of the hierarchy do not want you to slow down but, despite their public service announcements to the contrary, they want you to speed so you can get a ticket. Lastly, the reason for this preference is obvious. Speeding tickets are big business. They permit and justify the employment of an army of civil servants including police, their supervisors, court clerks, accountants, judges, secretaries, stenographers, bailiffs, computer operators, programmers, district attorneys, and more. At the same time, tickets provide the necessary revenue to pay all those gainfully employed voters. If the volume of issued tickets begins to drop, the whole system begins to crumble like a city in an earthquake.

Let us not forget that the revenue from tickets also spurs the economy. The municipalities find themselves spending ticket revenue on a multitude of manufactured items ranging from new courthouses, radar units and police cars to pens, pencils and file folders. These tickets also provide a massive amount of revenue for lawyers and insurance companies, who in turn, employ armies of support staff. If everyone stopped speeding tomorrow, our taxes would skyrocket and massive unemployment would begin. If our elected officials were honest they would tell you that you owe it to your country to speed.

Can't you just picture some politician standing at a podium while saying, "You folks must get out there and speed more so we can save this country from another recession." Perhaps our First Lady could sponsor a "Just Say Faster" program with catchy public service announcements done by famous race car drivers!

I don't know how we got into the mess where we are today and I certainly don't approve of it but the least I can do is try to give an equal chance to anyone who wants it, in their efforts to avoid the inevitable. Statistics tell us almost everyone will eventually get stopped for speeding at least once. Not all of them will get a speeding ticket though!

There are some laws that can't be broken. They are the laws of physics. If you choose to become a projectile and end up looking like the nose of a spent bullet, then shame on you. If weather, traffic or road conditions dictate a slower speed than you choose to go, stay off the road that I am on. There is no excuse for reckless driving. If you find yourself gripping the steering wheel just a little tighter and you are leaning a little forward in your seat, whatever the rush, it's not worth it. Many drivers perceive speeding as a challenging game they play with the police being the opposition. The fun goes away in a hurry if "the thrill of the chase" and poor judgment causes pain or death. Make all your trips safe ones, driven at a speed that is reasonable and prudent.

CHAPTER 2

The Truth About Cops & Traffic Stops

As difficult as this may be for the motoring public to believe, police are usually ambivalent when they pull a car over. In most cases they could care less if you drive away with a ticket in your pocket or not. You will notice I said "in most cases." If the officer has spent the last fifteen minutes dodging other traffic to catch up with you, or if he has caught you cruising along at a sedate 110 mph then it is entirely possible that he will be less than pleased with you.

Sometimes, no matter what you say or do, he or she will give you a little something to remember them by. I'm sure you realize that if there was a fool proof way of getting out of a ticket every time, to find out what it is would cost you a lot more than this book. In spite of this, it is important to remember, each time the driver is doomed to be ticketed, there are many more times when he has a much better fighting chance than he ever suspected.

Now that you know you do have that fighting chance of avoiding getting your speedometer certified by the nice, pleasant talking police person, it is time for the big surprise. Most people manage to talk themselves into a ticket, rather than talking themselves out of it. Speed enforcement is a lot like hunting wild game. When you first begin, you tend to shoot at anything you can, but the longer you are at it the better you get. As a result, you begin to pick and choose, waiting for the trophy and letting the average game walk by.

When game is very plentiful, you become more discriminating and when it is not, you tend to take any available shot. It is obvious that when hunting speeding cars, the ''game'' is quite plentiful. It is your responsibility, as the speeder, to be one of the just average ''game'' the hunting cop chooses to pass up. This book is designed to teach you how to try to be that average game most police officers choose to leave for another day.

It was not written to help you be your own lawyer in court. In fact, I intentionally tried to avoid delving into the lawyer's domain. If you do get a ticket, and want to fight it in court, pay the bucks and do it right. Hire a good attorney. The information contained in some parts of this book will, if done correctly, help that lawyer in his efforts to help you.

This book was written with the speeding Interstate driver in mind. Nevertheless, the information contained herein is of value anytime a person has dealings with a police officer. It could be a youth having his first police experience or the "professional driver" who just managed to jackknife his load of tomatoes in front of city hall. Regardless of the situation, if you know what makes a cop tick and how his mind works, you can minimize any damage and come out as good as possible, regardless of what the predicament is in which you may find yourself.

If I had to choose one part of this book as the most important, it would have to be this paragraph and the two that follow. So much is predicated on what a cop is and what makes a cop tick. Let's get one thing straight right now. We are not stupid. The Keystone Cops were comedy actors, not ticket writers. Most police are required to endure extensive schooling and take achievement tests before ever seeing the road. Most have had to beat out hundreds or even thousands of others on competitive entrance exams. It never ceased to amaze me how many people just naturally assume we lacked intelligence and, as a result, paid the price for their own stupidity by getting arrested or ticketed. Never underestimate your opponent however, once you know his weakness, pursue it.

A police officer's weakness is not stupidity, it is his personality. If he doesn't possess the standard police issue personality on the day he is sworn in, he will soon have it. There are two emotions that will rule his life. They are fear and a giant ego. Both will be with him constantly. He is "the man" and he must be "the man" whenever he is around anyone else, on duty or off. I have met some fellow officers who couldn't even let their guard down when they were in their own home and among their loved ones.

He is also constantly a target. That message is repeatedly brought home to him every time a brother officer is buried or injured. The same teletype machines that tell him what cars have been stolen and what kind of a license you have, also put out a message describing every incident where an officer is seriously injured. When one is killed in the line of duty, all funeral arrangements are also sent out on the teletype network. As a result, he is constantly reminded of the dangers of his profession. I do not mean to insinuate police officers are cowards. Quite the contrary is true. They live in almost constant fear and they must routinely overcome it. Other than the military, during war, what other job description faces the possibility of death so often? He must suspect every driver he approaches until the driver's actions permit him to lower his guard. Is it any wonder that these scared egotists succumb so often to alcoholism, heart disease, and suicide? Does it surprise anyone that their divorce rate is also so high? You may hate them or pity them but fear and ego are their weaknesses and your secret weapons. To avoid a ticket, you must reduce the man's fear as fast as possible and feed his ego as much as you can without making it too obvious what you are doing.

If you really want to escape without a ticket, it will probably be necessary to at some point, lie. If you decide to lie, for heavens sake, make it plausible! If the officer suspects you are not telling him the truth, then you will be certain to get a ticket. I don't mean to have you believe that sometimes an outlandish story won't work. It just has to be a possibility. Let me tell a short war story to illustrate. There was the proud owner of a brand new Cadillac that I was in the process of passing. As was my habit, I looked over at the driver. I couldn't help but notice his digital speedometer was plainly visible, and was reading 69 mph. I pulled him over intending to give him a warning but before I could say a word, he became insistent that his ''brand new'' car must have a faulty speedometer as he was certain his cruise control was on the speed limit, 55 mph. It was hard not to smile when I told him that perhaps he should turn in his drivers license as his eyesight seemed to be going fast. When I then told him his speedometer could be read from the driver's seat in my car, his face began to glow as he knew I had caught him in a bold lie. I also couldn't help but notice that the blush starting on his face was only slightly brighter than the red on his wife's as she tried her damndest not to burst out laughing. She failed. The man disobeyed one of the first rules of dealing with police. Never lie unless you are sure the lie is believable. Did the man get a ticket? You decide. After finishing this book, see if you come up with the same answer.

CHAPTER 3

The Care & Feeding Of
"Smokey The Bear"

Now that you know what emotions most affect cops and that those emotions effect the decisions they make as to whether to write a ticket or not, the rest of this book will address one of three subjects. Dealing with the cop's fear/ego will, of course, be a large portion of the book. We will also give you driving tips that should help you in not getting stopped in the first place. Can you think of a better way to avoid a ticket? It is also important to understand what weapons your enemy has in his arsenal. We will go into detail explaining the workings of Radar, Speed Computers, tactics and other police tools.

I have been repeatedly amused when I read literature about radar detectors or get a chance to eavesdrop on a conversation regarding the use of radar. You would think that truckers would have an intimate knowledge of police radar and how it works. After listening to them in truck stops for years, I can tell you that the majority of them have no real idea of what they are talking about when discussing radar. They have all become experts at mouthing the half truths and inaccuracies used in some radar detector advertisements and bias related articles in their trade magazines. It is sad too because understanding exactly what radar can or can't do is so important in knowing how to avoid being caught by it. Having that knowledge is also imperative if you are ever to understand what your detector is trying to tell you.

Let's start with the assumption that your rearview mirror has just been filled with two tons of police cruiser, containing two hundred pounds of determined law enforcer. The headlights are flashing and the light bar on top of the car is telling everyone in sight that you are into ''deep doggy doodoo'' as President Bush would say. Your first reaction is obvious. You pull your foot off of the accelerator and look at the speedometer. You then mouth the infamous line . . . ''Oh shit. . . .'' Which is the commonly used slang term meaning ''Oh goodness, I think that officer has just caught me speeding.'' You remember passing a similar police car going in the opposite direction about five minutes earlier and wonder if it is the same one.

There is a car in the driving lane to your right. You hit the brakes, pulling in behind it and point your trusty steed at the nearest shoulder. The far edge of that shoulder looks like it might be a little soft so you are careful not to pull too far to the right. Believe it or not, most of your actions since seeing the patrol car have already increased your chances of getting a ticket significantly. Hard to believe, isn't it? Well it's about to get a whole lot worse.

The officer walks up to your car and appears even less than his normal, congenial self. He snarls "license and registration" while spitting all over you with every "s." He informs you that you are getting a ticket for 74 in a 55, rips the paperwork out of your hand and storms back to his cruiser. About all you have time to notice is that his face is the color of your taillights and there is this funny little vein in his neck. Wait a minute! You were only doing 69 mph! You get out of your car to go back to talk to the nice officer with the funny red vein in his neck and you quickly realize that he not only won't listen to reason but wants to order you around. He keeps yelling "Get back in your *@#!!*$* car." Welcome to the real world.

By the time the officer comes back with your ticket in his hand, you are both fuming. You demand to see the radar read-out and he tells you that you can't. You tell him, in no uncertain terms that you were only going 69 mph and he responds by telling you that he won't testify on the side of the road. You demand to know his name and badge number, immediately forgetting his name but forever remembering the bath you got while finding out his badge was six sixty-six. That man has a way with the letter "S." As a last effort in regaining some of your dignity, you glare at him with your most "You can't intimidate me" look and growl "I'll see YOU in court!" He then takes back your paperwork and you find yourself following him directly to the judge. You're now entering the wonderful world of "taking bail" and you better have plenty of cash because the judge won't take a personal check.

What happened? All you were doing was speeding! Just what is that cop's problem! You're about to find out why a simple traffic stop turned into such a fiasco, by viewing the same incident through the eyes of the patrol man.

Traffic was moderate to heavy, a few minutes earlier when he first saw you about six miles back up the road. He was going in the opposite direction when he noticed your car approaching him in the passing lane. It was obvious your car was going faster than the other eight cars that were also in view. He activated a button attached to a cord that led to a box on his dash. The box had two LED displays that were lit up with the word "HOLD." As he pressed the button, his speed appeared in one of those boxes and a high-pitched whistle told him you would be a "keeper." Almost instantly he received a read-out in the other display port, labeled "violator." It lit up "74" and disappeared as the two of you passed each other. The high pitched tone was replaced with a lower one, as the radar chose it's next target and the LED again lit up with that car's lower speed.

Now all he had to do was catch you. He accelerated to about 90 mph and continued to the next crossover. Keep in mind that the two of you are now pulling away from each other at a speed of 164 mph and every foot must be regained by him after turning around. He would have liked to cut through the median but the highway department had installed a guide rail.

After entering the turn around, he had to wait for a clear spot in traffic. His car is standing still while yours continues to widen the gap by pulling 103.25 feet further away, every second. Like a drag race, he starts from a stopped position. Unlike a drag race, his "strip" is littered with other, slower moving cars. He must use his brakes every time he overtakes a car that fails to see him in time to pull to the right. He is fully aware that people on interstates spend far too little time looking in the rearview mirror. Even with his emergency lighting going, he knows his disk brakes are getting hot as people still fail to see him in time to get out of his way. To make matters worse, he overtakes a tractor trailer that is passing another truck and must wait for the truck to complete the pass before he can again accelerate after you.

Finally, you come into view ahead of him. What are you doing? You're still cruising along at 74 mph, in the passing lane, fat, dumb and happy. He follows you for another quarter of a mile with his lights on before you notice him. When he was unable to get your attention, at first, he pulled up fairly close to your back bumper, flashing his spotlight in your rearview mirror. As luck would have it, your car is overtaking Miss Sally Safedriver when you first notice you have police type company. She is traveling at a serene 53 mph.

About the time you are thinking. . . . "Oh shit," little Sally Safedriver has also noticed the cop and "everyone knows you slow down if a police man has his lights on" so she starts to brake. You wouldn't consider accelerating to complete the pass because there is a cop right behind you. What did you do? You slowed down even more to pull in behind Sally. Where does Officer Neckvein find himself? He is directly behind you standing with both feet on his brake pedal, trying to get his already overheated brakes to slow his rocket enough to avoid hitting you.

He then has to slow even further so as to be able to pull in behind you. When the dust clears and, after three swallows, his heart is back in its assigned position. He looks up to see he must again risk his life while talking to you because you are stopped so close to the driving lane. The cop knows he must now keep one eye on the oncoming traffic during any conversation with you. Is it any wonder he has no desire to stop and chat while the cars and trucks pass only a few inches from his corpulent tush? After chasing you for so long and then almost striking your car, is it not likely that his mood will turn sour?

There is more. As he then sits in his nice safe cruiser, taking deep breaths while waiting for his pulse to return to normal, he sees you getting out of your car. Again you are creating conflict for him. Are you going to get struck by a car or perhaps end up in some type of physical confrontation with him?

Do you have a weapon he does not know about? He knows that nothing good ever came from the violator leaving his car and he also knows that if anything bad happens, chances are he will be held accountable by his supervisors, the press and civil courts. Are you beginning to understand why he seems to be born without a sense of humor?

What could you have done to decrease your chances of getting a ticket? When you first saw the police car approaching, in the opposite direction, you could have slowed down and worked your way into the right lane, staying there for a while at a reduced speed. He would have had less difficulty catching you, would have known that you had slowed to a lower speed, and would have been able to pull in behind you without any danger.

You could have been more vigilant, watching behind you so as to see him approaching sooner. This is one time that radar detectors are a big help. If you had a unit and it went off as the police car was passing in the opposite direction, it should warn you to expect Officer Neckvein would be coming up behind you. Let's assume that, in spite of your best efforts, you find yourself next to Miss Safedriver when Officer Neckvein closes for the kill. The emergency lights are on and you know he wants you. What do you do?

If your first guess is "pull into the mall," Congratulations! You just failed. Very few things happen routinely that give the cop acid belly as much as people pulling into the mall. There are good reasons for this. Vehicles are going faster in the passing lane. You were. It is dangerous enough to pull out from the driving lane but much more dangerous from the left shoulder. The cop does it daily and knows how much more difficult it is. He also knows that your rear and side-view mirrors will be nearly useless as his car blocks your view. Murphy's Law, being what it is, he is willing to make book that . . . just as you pull out, a car will enter the passing lane from behind a slower moving truck. At night it is even worse. People approaching from the rear see the back of the police car, get confused, and more than one drunk has tried to go around everyone on the left with spectacular results. Always try to avoid entering the mall or median.

Your only other option is to accelerate and complete your pass, pulling well in front of Miss Safedriver. I know what you're thinking. "A cop is on my tail and this guy is telling me to speed up! He must think I'm crazy!" Not true. Think about it. The cop is behind you with his emergency lights on. If he is after you, HE HAS ALREADY CAUGHT YOU SPEEDING!!! If he is not after you, the sooner you get out of his way, the happier you all will be. Remember my comments about how often the off duty cops are stopped? This may be tough to believe, but the working officer pulling him over usually knows it is a cop before he ever walks up to the car. He knows it by the way the off duty cop pulls over. We are now going to teach you to pull over like a cop. Why bother? There are a number of reasons.

The conversation that takes place between the officer and the violator during the first thirty seconds is the most important. If you are going to be let off the hook, the cop will usually be considering it by then. The longer he talks to you, the better are your chances of driving away with only a warning. If he suspects you are an "off duty brother," his fear/anxiety level is coming down before any conversation has even taken place and he is more inclined to talk with you so as to find out if you are, in fact, a cop.

Off duty cops pull over in the safest way possible. To do otherwise is to irritate the uniformed Neanderthal that has chosen you for lunch. We are still working with the assumption that you are in the passing lane, next to another car, when you realize the police car is behind you. The first thing you do is raise your right hand up, bent at the elbow and move it left to right a couple of times. The cop now knows you have seen him and will be ready to slow down with you. You then turn on your right turn directional signal, telling him you are not going into the mall. Then, speed up enough to complete your pass, remembering there must be room for him to complete his pass too. The right turn directional signal will tell him what you are doing and why. The cop may choose to stay directly behind you or may drop into the right lane behind the other car. Regardless of his actions, YOU continue to pull over.

When you are safely in the driving lane in front of Miss Sally, whom you remember always slows down when the nice policeman is around, ease off the right side of the road, not stopping too fast. Give Officer Neckvein plenty of time to get his chariot off the road and slowed down. Regardless of the actions of Sally or the cop, make certain you don't slow down too quickly. Pull well off the road so the officer can park his car closer to the driving lane than yours. His car then becomes his protection from the traffic when he is talking to you.

If guide rails do not permit you to pull over far enough, try to pick a spot where they end and stop there. It is obvious that you shouldn't drive down the shoulder for a mile or two looking for a break in the rails but if there is one close by, use it.

If you are already in the driving lane when you are being pulled over, do it the same way. You wave, put on the right turn indicator and make sure you don't stop too fast. Remember, traffic behind the two of you presents a danger to him and you don't want to make a "Smokey Sandwich" by braking too fast.

At night, it is very important to immediately turn on your interior light. Do not start looking through the glove box for your paper work. After putting the car in park, turn off your radio and CB. Put out your cigarette or cigar in the ashtray, not out the window. If you are chewing gum, put that in the ash tray. If you are wearing sunglasses, take them off. Roll your window all the way down and sit still with both hands on the steering wheel. You now are ready to talk to the nice policeman.

Surprise! His face is now a normal color and you can't even see that vein in his neck. Negotiations are now much more likely to happen and should be about ready to begin. You have a very good chance at success. This time, everything you have done since noticing the officer, has reduced your chances of a ticket rather than increasing them. The cop is fairly comfortable with his situation and feels, more or less, safe in your presence. It will soon be time to start feeding his ego. But first let's explain to you why your actions were so important.

Turning on the interior light was obvious. He feels safer if he can see you and you can't see him. By not bouncing all over the place, or going into the glove box, he knows there is less chance you will be holding a gun in your hand when he walks up to you. With both of your hands on the steering wheel, your body language is saying "I present no danger to you, I am your friend." If you were still sitting in the front seat, going through your pockets or trying to dig your wallet out, the appearance is quite different.

If you try to exit your car, the appearance is one of imminent danger to the cop. Never exit your car unless you first ask the cop for permission. Stay seated with your hands on the wheel until he approaches. Turning off your radios, having the window open before he gets there, and getting rid of your gum or smoking materials are courtesies that many people don't bother doing. See that you do.

It may be a few minutes before he walks up to you. Don't act nervous and start fidgeting. He is most likely running your plate through whatever computers are available to him to see if the registered owner, or the car is wanted. This requires radio transmissions and a wait before he gets his reply. The amount of time depends on the whims of his dispatcher and how backed up the computers are. Just stay put and don't be twisting around looking back at him. He will get to you in good time. You don't want to present the appearance of being in a hurry.

Have you ever watched dogs playing or a nature film showing a wolf pack interacting? There is always a "top dog" and the others show their subservience by rolling over and displaying their throat. Their reward is not getting their butt kicked. I guess you could say that your demeanor up to this point should be similar to the dog showing his throat. It is going to get worse before it gets better. If your macho ego does not permit playing up to the cop's ego then, all I can say is enjoy your ticket, but don't blame me when you get one.

On the other hand, if you have minimal acting skills and are willing to swallow your pride for a few minutes, you just might beat the cop at his own game. Oh! Wouldn't the taste of that success be sweet? There is nothing keeping you from cursing the cop and his ancestral heritage, after you pull away, if it makes you feel better. For the time being, swallow your pride. Most violators already try to play this game but do it in the wrong way. Listening to some guy who could easily twist even my economy size frame into a pretzel, as he tries to break the world record for inserting "Sir" into a conversation, can be entertaining but not impressive. Swallowing your pride for a few minutes won't kill you and could help you immensely, if done right.

There is another good reason for not having your license and registration ready before he asks. When he does ask for it you will have a chance to talk to him while you look for it. Before we begin teaching you what to say to the nice police type person, let's finish up a few more points that we haven't touched on with respect to the first scenario. You remember the less than pleasant encounter with officer Neckvein?

There was some disagreement with respect to how fast you were going. When you looked down at your speedometer, you were going 69 mph. It is very common for the violator to believe he was going a few miles slower. After years of this happening, I believe I know why. Obviously, the policeman caught you on his radar at a different time and place but that is not what causes the problem. I have been behind cars, clocking them with a certified speedometer, and when stopped, the drivers almost always insisted they were going four or five mph slower than I knew they were traveling. This happened so often, and with my using different police cars, that it made me wonder. It was a repeated source of ill feelings on the part of the violator as he was willing to believe he was speeding but not at the speed I told him he was going. The answer was so simple, I felt quite foolish when I finally figured it out.

When you see a police car, even if you are traveling at the speed limit, your first reaction is to lift the foot that's on the accelerator. At slower speeds there is not a noticeable change but at interstate speeds, the speedometer almost instantly shows a four to five mph reduction. When you look down and see that slower speed, nothing the cop can say will sway your conviction that you "just weren't going that fast." The high engine RPMs causes this and it's amazing how quick the speed drops. You will learn to use this to your advantage in another part of this book.

Let's cover just a couple more points regarding our fictitious stop before we move along to other things. Remember I mentioned sunglasses? Cops often wear them but you make sure you take yours off. It is another small "victory" that you can grant the cop. Notice how nervous you are, having to look into his "mirrors?" Well, we don't want to make the little officer nervous too, now do we? Remember the old movies where the interrogations were always held? The suspect would be sitting on a stool with a bright light in his face. The cops got to stand around in the dark, snarling questions and blowing cigarette smoke in the suspect's face. Sooner or later the poor guy would break down, confessing everything. Oh, for the good old days.

To be serious for a moment. There is a definite psychological advantage at being able to see your opponent's eyes when he cannot see yours. It is one more way you can make the officer comfortable with his surroundings. He will be feeling just a little more in control and subsequently less fearful.

Look straight into his "mirrors." If he is not wearing sunglasses, look straight into his eyes. That will help you appear more of a human, rather than another number. You will want the officer to feel empathy toward you so he won't want to write you a ticket.

Last of all, let's touch on the famous line "See you in court." Any person who would mouth those words to a cop must:

A) Be divorcing him
B) Is a masochist
C) Measures his IQ in single digits
D) Just doesn't know any better.

I will give you the benefit of the doubt and assume you are in the "D" category but don't let it happen again. By mouthing off to the cop with that particular gem, you have created a situation where your over-paid and underworked lawyer is going to have a much more difficult time negotiating a reduction or dismissal for you. Here is how you have just blown almost any chance you still had for a satisfactory outcome regarding the ticket:

When you told the cop "See you in court," you told him much more than the fact you were unhappy with the situation. He knew that already. You told him that he did not have to concern himself with another officer contacting him on your behalf, asking for a reduction or dismissal. In spite of claims to the contrary, this is a routine occurrence in many, if not most jurisdictions. You also told him that you did not have the political clout to get the ticket fixed. People who have such clout simply consider the issuance of a ticket as a minor delay and never get upset.

Worse than that, you just showed your hand to an expert poker player who knows the game you are playing much better than you ever will. If you choose not to fold (plead not guilty) he will be able to take you to the cleaners. The main reason most tickets get reduced, or won by the defendant in court is poor memory on the part of the cop.

When you get a ticket, chances are you will remember almost everything about it for years to come. You must, because every time someone found out I was a State Trooper, they would have to tell me all about the ticket they got. Talk about boring! To the cop, you are just one traffic stop out of the hundreds or thousands he does every year. With a little luck on your part, he will have forgotten all about you by the end of the day. Want to beat a ticket? Have the officer testify he can't remember what direction you were traveling and watch what happens to the case. Get my drift?

When someone says "See you in court," the officer knows he can expect to file additional paperwork with the court and may even go to trial. He goes directly back to his car and takes copious notes about the stop, noting everything from the weather, to the clothing you were wearing. He may even have quotes he can attribute to you. Included in those notes will be a comment about your attitude. If you had kept your mouth shut, the only thing he would have had to refresh his memory would have been the preprinted boxes on the ticket. Do you think your lawyer would be able to do much for you now? I doubt it. As I mentioned before, most people manage to talk themselves into a ticket. There are many more things that you should avoid saying but we will cover that later.

So what do you say to get out of a ticket? I am sure you have figured out that it is your total attitude and deportment that most effects the ultimate outcome. For your benefit I will go over some of the tricks that have been tried on me, some with better results than others. What you choose to try, if you choose anything, is your business. What would work for one person would never work for another. Believe it or not, I have let people go just because they did not try to con me but simply asked that the ticket not be written and honestly gave the reasons why.

In fact, if your intention is to plead guilty and not use a lawyer, your best chance of getting out of the ticket is total honesty. Acknowledge that you were going too fast, explain the reasons why, (even if the reason was you were just plain bored), don't try to excuse your actions and then ask the cop to show mercy, giving the reasons why he should.

It is best if you read and digest the whole book and after doing so, decide what you will do if the time comes. It is more important that you decide in advance what you are going to say, than the content of what you choose to say. By that I mean you should have decided long before you were stopped what ploy you planned to use. If you wait until you get stopped, it will be too late to start planning your reasons or excuses, regardless of how quick you think in emergencies.

When that cop comes up to the car, it is likely he will have no desire to converse with you any more than will be necessary. He is no fool. If he lets you go, he has to find another victim to replace you. He is also in control of the conversation and will try to keep it as brief as possible. Why? Simple. If you don't have a chance to give him reason not to write the ticket, then the ticket will get written.

You will have about thirty seconds (more or less) to plead your case. The longer the conversation lasts, the better your chances become. Don't give one syllable answers. If you can talk while getting out your license and registration, so much the better. He can't leave until you give it to him. Now do you see why you should not have it ready and waiting for him?

Believe it or not, there is even a right and wrong way to look for your paperwork. When he asks you for it, for heavens sake, don't ask "Why!" Look him straight in the face and say, "Of course." If you don't like that line you can substitute "Sure" or "Certainly." I'm sure, by now, you know why you should do this. Like bread crusts to the pigeons you are throwing little pieces of bird feed that helps reduce his fear and inflate his ego.

There is another reason for this particular, subtle little ploy. If someone is going to give the cop a hard time, it usually begins with the violator trying to refuse to relinquish his paperwork. He may insist on asking the officer why he was pulled over. Are we beginning to describe your last traffic stop before reading this book? By letting the cop know he will be getting your paperwork without a problem, you are one more little step closer to driving away with just a warning. Sooner or later he will tell you why you were stopped. Don't ask.

What comes next? Simple. You tell the nice Cossack where you think you will most likely find the tax receipts your state has so gratuitously bestowed on you in return for their annual chunk of bucks. You look at him and say, "My license and registration are in my wallet.'' Then reach for your pocket AFTER BREAKING EYE CONTACT!!! If you continue to look into his face, you are telegraphing the possibility that he is about to be blown to hell by your concealed gun. Don't ask me why, hell, I'm no psychologist, but it's true. Maybe it is the combination of our being taught to look exactly where we want to shoot, at the same time your hands will be removed from our view, and placed in an area where concealed guns are most often carried. I can only tell you that the hair will be starting to rise on the back of his neck until your hand and wallet are back in his view.

If you need to look in the glove box, look back at the officer and tell him what you intend to do. ''The registration is in the glove box'' or ''I carry the reg. in there.'' The exact words aren't as important as the act of letting him know your intent. You then break eye contact again before starting to reach over. Once you get the paperwork out of the glove box, leave the little door open. Why not? You will have to put the paperwork away sooner or later and it will be still another small crumb to the pigeon. Your action will be telegraphing the message, ''Take a good look officer, I have nothing to hide from you.''

The opposite is true if you are going into a console between the seats. Leave the top wide open while you are in it but then close it as soon as you can. Why? It's too easy for you to reach back into the console and come out with a gun. Unless there are two officers, he won't be able to see inside from his position, standing next to you. Be sure to ''ca-

31

sually'' mention to the cop what you are doing before actually doing it.

I have always gotten a kick out of the people who have tried to ''show respect'' by repeatedly calling me ''Sir.'' It always sounded so phony. Unless you happen to be in the military, the term ''sir'' is no longer commonly used and sounds so out of place. I know you mean well but limit your ''Sir.'' to one time, if you must use it at all. There is a better alternative that is more likely to get the desired results. Take the time to find out which particular police tribe your nemesis represents and then call him by his proper title. Is he a member of a county sheriff's office or does he belong to a highway patrol? Is he part of a state police outfit or is he a local cop? What is his rank?

I worked very hard to become a trooper (state police) and even harder for the stripes that signified I was a supervisor. If someone took the trouble to notice those stripes and called me sergeant or sarge, it usually had a very positive effect.

Again, I can read most of your minds. You are thinking ''Just how the deuce am I supposed to find out what to call some cop that has just pulled me over?'' It's like riding a bicycle. Once you know how, it's really quite easy. Unless you have been pulled over by a cop in an unmarked car, you will be able to see the decal or writing on his driver's side door when he opens it up to get out. Just keep looking in your side view mirror until he exits the car. I grant you that the writing will be backward but you should be able to at least determine if it says "Sheriff," "State Police" or "Highway Patrol." Most of the time it will be one of those three. Many of the states have color-coded cars but you can't always depend on that. At any rate, if it is a State Police patrol, call him "Trooper." If it is a County Sheriff patrol, call him "Deputy." All others are "Officer." Do not mix up a "State Police" patrol with a "Highway Patrol." If it says "Highway Patrol," call him Officer. This little trick can backfire so, be certain of the type of agency before greeting him with it. Should you call a Deputy Sheriff a "Trooper" or a Highway Patrolman "Deputy," you won't be gaining points, but losing them! There is much more inter-departmental jealousy than most "outsiders" realize.

You can also tell by looking at the uniform, what type of cop he is. Each agency has a shoulder patch that is unique to their outfit. Some people make it a hobby of collecting the different patches and some of those patches are quite attractive. If you see one that is unique or unusual, ask the cop about it. How's that for getting his mind off ticket writing?

Regardless of the agency he belongs to, look for stripes on the upper part of his shirt or jacket sleeves. If he has three or more stripes, it is a safe bet he is some kind of sergeant and you should greet him with that title. If you see only two stripes, chances are he is corporal. Is this getting a little confusing? Believe me, it will be worth the effort to read this part over until you have it "down pat." Here is a guide that might help:

1. If his sleeve has 3 or more stripes, call him Sergeant or Sarge.

2. If his sleeve has 1 or 2 stripes, call him Corporal.

3. If you see no stripes and he is a member of the State Police, call him Trooper.

4. If you see no stripes and he is a member of a County Sheriff's department, call him Deputy.

5. All others and if in doubt, call him Officer.

As you have noticed, we have been referring to officers in the masculine term. Now might be a good time to tell you a little about the women who have been entering the police ranks in more and more numbers every year. The traffic ticket game is the same, regardless of the gender of your opponent. You should treat her exactly the same as you would a male cop. The fear/ego connection is still very much there and the female officer should be manipulated in the exact same manner that works so well with the male. If anything, the fear portion of her personality is even stronger, not because she is more in fear for her safety but because many female cops carry a fear of failing by making a serious mistake and having others blame that failure on their womanhood. Their desire is to be accepted for what they are, the equal of the men. Most of them neither want nor expect special treatment and resent it when they are treated differently. Just as the male officer puts on his uniform and becomes "the man," the female also strives to be construed in that same vein and pictures herself that way.

The problem is not so much with female cops as it is the reaction of males to them. In our society, since Adam & Eve, the male has viewed himself as clan leader. The female was someone for him to protect, watch over, and pursue for a sexual liaison. You must realize that when a female officer is working, she thinks of herself, not as a woman, but as a cop ("the man"). If you think you can "sweet talk the little girl," you will very soon find out she has no patience for your foolishness. Try to use the same techniques that worked so well in the bar last week and she may hand you your head on a platter. If you had a date with her and brought flowers, you would be rewarded with the same reaction as any other woman. Offer her the same bouquet of flowers at a traffic stop and she just might make you eat them.

Consequently, there are a few extra rules to follow when dealing with a lady cop. Don't give her your big toothy smile that shows off your caps so well! Don't try to pick her up. You're just not that handsome. Don't call her "Miss," "M'am," "Dear," "Honey" or even "Sir." If you call her by her title (Trooper, Deputy, Officer, Sergeant, etc.) you will be on the right track. If you find you just can't keep yourself from flirting, you will soon realize she resents being reminded of her femininity at that time and your reward will be one irritated cop. The best advice I can give is just try to ignore the fact they are females.

Some of the cops I have worked with who happened to be female were dedicated, outstanding police officers and some of them were arrogant overbearing jerks. Is that not exactly what we find when we look at the male officers?

CHAPTER 4

Tricks & Deceptions

As long as we have just covered how men should react to women cops, is it not fair to now cover how women should react to men cops? These next few paragraphs are for ladies. In reality, you women don't deserve any special space because the deck is already stacked in your favor. You see, the comment I made about society depicting the man as the protector also affects the relationship that exists between a male cop and a female violator. Yes, it is true that most male cops are predisposed to letting a pretty female go. Now all those rumors are official! Showing a well-turned leg and unbuttoning the top button of the blouse, has often worked in the past.

There is bad news for you on the horizon though. Because the last few years have seen a plethora of law suits and allegations of sexual harassment against police officers, ladies have found that, when it comes to getting a ticket, they are the victims of their own cries for sexual equality. More and more male officers are writing tickets to females they would otherwise be inclined to let off. Yet the ticket gets written because they fear a false allegation of sexual harassment or even a law suit, should they let you go. If the cop writes a woman a ticket, and is later accused of stopping her in the hopes of a sexual liaison, he has the ticket to show as his legitimate reason for stopping her. If he lets her go and then is accused, the woman's accusation will be viewed differently. As hard as this is for some officers to believe, there are many people out there who just don't like being stopped by cops and make a complaint if they feel they are stopped for an invalid reason. I remember one incident when a young lady's boyfriend initiated a complaint because the trooper complimented the girl on her appearance. The officer couldn't imagine someone being offended just because he casually mentioned to the fiancé that she had a dynamite body. When interviewed about the incident, his reaction was "Some people just can't take a compliment!"

Fear not dear ladies! You still have your secret weapon! It works for both the beauty queen and the ugly duckling. It works for the matron as well as the debutante. I don't have to tell most of you what it is. I'm sure you already know. For the benefit of all the men who are reading these paragraphs, the secret weapon is. . . . (would the drummer please be kind enough to give us a rolling intro. . . .)

TEARS

Nothing melts the big brave cop's heart like an avalanche of tears. Keep in mind, you can't cry too much. The more you bawl, the better your chances of being let off! Many of you ladies make the mistake of trying to be brave, only sniffling or weeping softly into your hanky. Now is not the time to keep a stiff upper lip or maintain your dignity. Good grief, there is the possibility of a ticket in the balance! Start bellowing like a cow and turn on those water works any way you can!!!

Don't wait too long either. It's a lot easier for the cop to let you go with a warning BEFORE he says you are going to get a ticket than it is for him to admit you have managed to change his mind. Remember how important the first thirty seconds of conversation is? If you are going to use crying as a defense, you should be doing it by then.

Do you consider this an affront to your dignity? Have I insulted you? Look, you wanted to know what works and bawling your eyes out is very effective. I have often wondered if it might work even better for a man! I can just see the reaction of the cop when the burly trucker's beer belly starts bouncing uncontrollably as he is blubbering like a baby! I know what my reaction would have been. LET ME OUT OF HERE!!!!!

If some of you ladies are thinking that you just paid big bucks for this book, only to have me tell you what you already know, take heart, there is more. I like to refer to it as "The Broken Bones Corollary." Now I grant you this one is tacky. It is dishonest and underhanded. It is totally without dignity and is, in one word, reprehensible. I've got everyone's interest again, haven't I?

The concept of the broken bones corollary is really quite simple. If bawling won't elicit enough sympathy from the officer, then you must increase that sympathy factor to the degree that you overload his senses. This one should even work on female cops, who are generally immune to the crocodile tears.

Much has been made of the police officers who callously do nothing when encountering a battered wife. In reality, this is not the case yet because cops are so sensitive to the allegation, you can use it to your advantage. Regardless of the criminal offense, cops are not permitted to make an arrest without either physical proof (evidence) or a complainant, especially if the criminal act was not witnessed by them. When they get called to the Thumper residence and find Mr. Thumper drinking beers in the game room, nothing is then happening.

They interview Mr. Thumper's wife, and she most frequently tells the cop, "I just want him out of the house," yet she will sign no formal complaint so her husband can be arrested. The cop can not compel a wife to testify against her husband and so he can't prove that Mr. Thumper is the culprit. His only recourse is do nothing but tell the wife to call again if she changes her mind. It would be very convenient at that time, for everyone involved, if the cops were given the right to banish a person from his legal domicile however, the civil libertarians would become a trifle uneasy about giving cops those kinds of powers. Much as I hate to admit it, I have to agree with them on this one.

Does it seem like we have just digressed from our subject matter a smathering? Not really. I'm sure some of the sharper readers have already figured out exactly how the broken bones corollary works. Through your weeping, wailing and gnashing of teeth, you tell the nice officer that your husband, father, uncle, or some other male type father figure said he would beat you if you got a speeding ticket. Be sure he understands that the beating will occur if the ticket is for speeding. This gives the cop the option of giving you a ticket for a lesser charge, such as no taillights. He gets his scratch, or number, as they are called, and drives away feeling he has done his good turn for the day. You just might drive away with a smirk on your face and a ticket in your pocket that will cost you much less in court and will not increase your car insurance.

Do not use a boy friend or fiancé as the bad guy because they are much less likely to work. The cop will feel that he might be saving you from the mistake of a horrible marriage if he gives you the ticket. Perhaps you will see what a cad and bounder you are with and dump him. I told you cops were not stupid. I forgot to mention that years of driving around by themselves tends to give them one hell of an imagination. Know your enemy and learn his weaknesses. Once you know your enemy, you may come up with your own plan for winning that might even be better for you than the ones this book describes.

With that in mind, I feel it is also important that

you understand why the broken bones corollary is so apt to work. Because the cop is sensitive to the television documentaries and news coverage that almost always portrays him as unwilling to take action with respect to domestic violence, he would find it almost impossible to even indirectly cause a spousal beating.

We are not all saints and there are plenty of cops who use their wives as punching bags. You will find those kind of people in all walks of life. As strange as it may seem, every spouse beater with whom I have had contact, tried to rationalize their actions in almost exactly the same way. His wife is different and deserves the beatings. It is HER FAULT. She drives him to do it. It wouldn't happen with any other woman. As asinine as this may sound, even a cop who beats his own wife will be inclined to let you off if he really thinks his writing a ticket will cause you a beating.

As if the ladies don't have the odds stacked enough in their favor, when it comes to getting out of tickets, there is even another angle for them to work. I always would be impressed by any woman who brought this one off because it is designed to destroy any lingering fear the cop might have at the same time it builds his ego to a crescendo. Where did we ever get the idea they were the weaker sex?

Let's call this one "The Trembling Corollary." It is quite easy to use and can often be incorporated with the bawling ruse, so as to give the cop a double whammy. You simply feign terror! As the cop walks up to your car, poor little you seems to be shaking like a leaf. When you were a little girl, didn't your mother tell you the policeman would throw you in jail if he caught you being bad? Now here is the big bad boogie man, and he just caught you speeding. You have never been so close to a real policeman before and "My God! Is that a real gun?" Why you're just so terrified of that larger than life cop!

It is important for your voice to be cracking and your breathing must sound like you are on the verge of hyper-ventilating. If he asks you what is the matter tell him how scared you are of him. If he asks if you are O.K., tell him, "No," you are in fear of him! He will then try to tell you how you don't have to be afraid of him but it won't work. You're going to point out how you are so scared because he is going to give you a speeding ticket and you just don't know what to do. How could any self-respecting cop go home to his family after spending the day terrifying sweet little you? Why, it would be down right cruel to give you a ticket under those circumstances.

Why does this stratagem work so often? The cop views himself as a twentieth century knight in shining armor. He is protector of the weak and defeater of the bad guys. Now just how do you think Sir Lancelot is going to feel when one of the weak "little people" he has sworn to protect and defend is so scared of him? Is he going to reinforce your fearful attitude by giving you a ticket, or will he be inclined to show how mistaken you are by letting you go?

The real beauty of this one is the way the violator uses roll playing to make the cop do her bidding while, at the same time, and with the same tools, she addresses the fear/ego cop personality. By assuming the role of defenseless maiden, she almost forces the cop to respond to her "mistaken fear" by becoming her "protector." While doing this, any fear the cop had is gone because her actions represent no threat to him at all. As her "protector," the cop's ego is inflated to the proportions of a super nova. After assuming that role, the cop would face a moral dilemma if he were to still write a ticket.

It is important that you convey to the cop that the accepted behavior for him will be to let you go because then he would be proving to you that your fear was unwarranted. You must link the fear of the cop with the issuing of the speeding ticket.

Enough of giving help to just the ladies. Let's now cover points applicable to both men and women. There are a couple of tricks that are often tried which everyone should avoid. The first one that comes to mind is, "I am speeding because I am sick." I realize that it makes no sense at all, yet it is one of the most common fabrications people try. The response from the cop is usually an offer to call an ambulance for you and a tow truck for your car. Talk about calling your bluff in a big way! Don't forget. He will still have plenty of time to write the ticket while he waits for the emergency vehicle.

As can be expected, the violator usually declines the offer of an ambulance as he is "not that sick." The cop, who knows from the very beginning that you were trying to put him on, will then point out how you might be too sick for him to permit you to continue to drive your car. You are now placed

44

in the position of having to convince the cop you are not really very sick at all. Any chance you had of not getting a ticket is gone and to add insult to injury, the cop will be laughing at you while he writes it.

If someone else is in the car, it is just as big a mistake to claim they are sick. That makes a little more sense but still won't hold much water at trying to get out of a ticket. I always had the same response when a driver claimed someone else in the car was sick. With my voice dripping sarcasm, I would glare at the driver and comment, "At the speed you were going, and the way you were driving, I would be surprised if your passengers felt well!" I would then offer the services of our local ambulance corps to take them to the hospital if they couldn't wait while the ticket was written. The only taker, in twenty years, was a young doctor from New York City who claimed his wife was sick. He would have been better off to just take the ticket and be quiet. I know the ambulance ride alone cost him more than the ticket. It didn't surprise me at all when the folks in the emergency room could find nothing wrong with Mrs. Smartmouth.

If Dr. Smartmouth was expecting the hospital bill would be waived as a "professional courtesy" he was in for another surprise. Once I told the Emergency Room Doctor the real reason for our little side trip, he was a smathering less than amused. I would love to have been a mouse in the lady's pocket when she finally got her husband alone. After all the tests the Emergency Room Doctor put her through, that little family get-together must have been a riot!

Something that often works is to claim you have to relieve yourself. (Did I mention this book might become a tad tacky in parts?) There are some big advantages to this hoax. For starters, how could the cop call your bluff? I was always tempted to look a man straight in the eye and say, "Prove it!" Wouldn't that have made a great story for the guys at the driver's next bowling banquet? Occasionally, I would point at some thick woods or bushes next to the interstate and say, "Go ahead, while I write the ticket." Only once did a man have the perfect response as he looked up at me with a pained expression and asked, "Do you have any toilet paper?" I had to let the guy go. I just had to. The truth is, if I believed the person was telling the truth, I would often let them go so they could answer nature's call as quickly as possible.

Just as everything else involving a traffic stop has a right or wrong way, I think you would be disappointed if I didn't point out there is a proper way to use the "Potty Ploy." As in every other effort, speed is of the essence (no pun intended). You have to begin before the officer even reaches the side of your car. As he is walking up to your car, twist your head around and out the window and say "Officer, if you're going to give me a ticket, please follow me to the nearest restroom first? I honestly don't think I can hold it much longer." If you were really in distress, would you be sitting there, casually waiting for the cop to approach? No, of course not.

You should also be getting painful cramps while looking for your license and registration. They will bend you over and cause you to groan pitifully. It would help if you can keep a straight face while looking up at the officer and whining, "I don't think I can hold it much longer," a couple or more times. Each time a cramp bends you over, you will beg the nice defender of the little people, to let you continue to the nearest restroom.

Don't expect him to grant your request. Unless the next public restrooms are very close, he won't follow you for a number of reasons. For instance, what happens if you continued to speed with him behind you, and then had an accident? He might be subject to civil liability.

Notice I did NOT tell you to ask the officer not to write the ticket. People who are really in distress don't care about anything but the mileage to the nearest rest area. Be certain you ask the officer where the nearest restroom is located and can't he, at least meet you there. In most cases, he will not want to follow you and, if he believes you, will not want to keep you sitting there while he writes a ticket. His only other recourse is to let you go with a warning.

If you choose to try the "Potty Ploy," there are a few more do's and don'ts. It is very important for you to keep a close watch over rest areas, service areas, and exits with service stations. If you just motored past Exit #99, only three miles back, and Exit #99 just happens to have about a dozen or more public restrooms, the cop will know his patrol area, will know you are lying, and you will be getting a ticket.

Assume for a moment that nature was calling you, in no uncertain terms. How fast would you accelerate to in the hopes of finding relief? That is about the same speed you should be going if you expect the "Potty Ploy" to work. If your car is a blur, and the cop sees you driving like a maniac then I doubt anything will work.

Regardless of whether you get a ticket or not, it is very important to stop at the next restroom and then behave yourself for the next fifteen miles or so. Can you imagine your position if you were pulled over again by the same officer, somewhere past the rest stop. Your only defense, and it would be a near miracle if you pulled it off, would be to claim another intestinal attack of diarrhea and ask directions to the nearest motel as you "Just can't go any further today."

So what else has worked well? Have you ever been passed by a reckless driver you suspected was drunk? You would mumble to yourself, "I'd like to see a cop right now. That man ought to get a ticket." Here is your chance. If you are speeding and someone passes you, note at least the state and some numbers on the vehicle's license plate. Then drive slightly slower than him, keeping him in sight as long as possible while still traveling slightly slower. When another vehicle passes you, repeat the process, again noting part of the plate and a vague description of the vehicle. It can be a car but tractor trailers work best. (Sorry Mr. Trucker, but you can get back at those four wheelers by playing the same game.) Try to keep the guy within sight but ahead of you by a quarter mile or so. As Mr. Policeman latches onto you, it is time to pull the "Erotic Driver Ploy."

Again I can read your thoughts. You're thinking "Doesn't he mean erratic driver ploy?" The answer is No! Now you just pay attention! Sex sells books! Just how do you expect anyone to be able to insert a few sexy, steamy, passionate paragraphs in a book about driving? Good grief! The best I have managed so far is a discourse on how to pretend you have to go to the bathroom. I'm writing this thing and if I want to call it the "Erotic Driver Ploy" then that's my privilege!

To give credit where it is due, there was a toll booth operator on the New York State Thruway who would report "an erotic driver" when someone would be exiting and made a reckless driving complaint about another driver. I don't know if he did it on purpose or not but the troopers would become nearly hysterical every time the fellow used the radio to notify the post car. How our imaginations would run wild as we would search in vain for each erotic driver, only to be disappointed in finding just another drunk or a half asleep state legislator on his way home from the state capital with his foot firmly inserted in the carburetor.

Here is how to utilize the "Erotic Driver Ploy." As the officer approaches your car, you say "Am I glad to see you!" Now that alone will tend to throw him off balance. I'm sure you will agree with me that not very many officers are greeted in that manner when they pull someone over for speeding.

The cop will already be viewing you as one of the "ones that got away." Anyone who starts a conversation like that will NOT be a routine traffic stop.

Before he has a chance to ask for your license and registration, tell him how you have been trying to raise an officer on channel 9 or 19 of your CB radio (assuming you have a CB). Don't worry about being caught in this lie. Any cop who works the interstate knows how unreliable those CB radios are and how easy it is for a message to be covered by someone else transmitting at the same time. If you have a cellular telephone, tell him you were just trying to get the operator to connect you with the police. You then tell him all about this crazy driver that can't be more than a couple of miles ahead of you and you believe the driver has to be drunk.

You point out how the other driver not only went flying by you but was tailgating and weaving. When you tell him you can describe the vehicle and know part of the license plate, the cop is placed in a quandry. You then ask him to "call ahead" on his radio so someone can catch this highway menace. You have just put the officer into more of a quandry. When he tells you that he pulled you over for speeding you say, "Of course, I was trying to keep that nut in view until I could get one of you guys; but I was afraid to get too close or go any faster so he was pulling away. He still can't be more than a few miles or so ahead of us." The officer has just gone from quandry to dilemma.

Even if the officer chooses to entirely ignore your story, and he won't, with your ticket will come the satisfaction of knowing you have ruined his day. As he walks away, he will be very concerned that you will have the ability to make him look like a callous buffoon in court. Events may even result in his being brought up on charges. Again I can read the reader's mind. You are thinking "How did I do that?" You have a short memory. Have you forgotten already about the cop's vivid imagination? Years of experience have shown him that, no matter what decision he makes, it often comes back to haunt him.

Actually, it's almost certain you will avoid the ticket altogether as most cops would choose not to tempt fate. Based on the multiple of quandries you have created, it is in the cop's best interest to just let you go so he can speed off after the "bad guy" you have reported. In most cases, that is exactly what will happen. It's explanation time again isn't it?

Other than being killed or injured, the one thing a cop fears most is his reputation or image being destroyed. In this melodrama we are dealing with a different kind of fear, the fear of failure or public ridicule. It places the cop in a most precarious position. His big ego just cannot handle accusations of incompetence or malfeasance. The same cop who thinks nothing of eating in front of twenty people at Big Bertha's Diner and walking out without paying, would be mortified if accused of failing to do his duty. It's a strange world we live in, isn't it? Here is how your conversation affected the cop. . . .

Quandry #1 - To ticket you is unfair if by doing so, he lets a more serious violator go.

Quandry #2 - You had a "quasi-legitimate" reason for speeding. You tried to keep the "bad guy" in sight but did not duplicate the "bad guy's" violation as you were not going as fast.

Quandry #3 - Anyone can claim someone else was driving recklessly but by being able to describe the other vehicle, including a partial plate, the officer now knows that should that other car cause an accident up the road, you are living proof the cop had a chance to "do his duty" and chose to just sit there, giving you a ticket.

Quandry #4 - What if you make a complaint to the cop's boss or the press claiming he took no action? Complaints, even though unfounded, cause the cop aggravation he doesn't want.

Quandry #5 - You are reporting a possible drunk driver! Which is more important, a speeding ticket or getting a drunk off the road that might kill someone?

Quandry #6 - You asked the officer to radio ahead yet, in most cases he knows there is no one to whom he can call. Most of the time, there are very few cops in any one area. If he tells you he did this, he can just picture driving up on a ten car fatal accident a few miles down the road, involving the car you described. He knows you would also pull up on the same accident. If he had just given you a ticket, wouldn't you tell the nice television crew all about how you "told the officer, and he did nothing?"

Quandry #7 - He doesn't know you are lying. He will be concerned that you might plead not guilty and relate in traffic court how you got a ticket for trying to be a good citizen, only to find the cop would do nothing.

Don't worry about the officer stopping the other car or truck. You are just a civilian and should not be expected to know a drunk driver from a sober one. Unless the cop sees the other vehicle commit a violation of law, there is nothing he can do except make sure the driver is not drunk. In the meantime, you will be long gone.

Shall we move on to still another trick? I already told you that cops don't give other cops tickets. In spite of this knowledge, NEVER CLAIM TO BE A POLICE OFFICER! We have our own jargon and in most state jurisdictions, it is a criminal offense to claim to be a cop. In addition, it is the rare individual that could make such a claim and be able to convince the cop of his sincerity. Police just have their own way of talking and acting. If you try it, you will end up in very hot water.

You might want to try what I call the "Lack of Guilt by Association Ploy." It works because police also try to refrain from giving tickets to the families of other cops. Before the officer gets your license in his hot little hand, mention that you are either traveling to or from you brother's house in an adjoining state. Also mention that your brother just happens to be a cop. Better yet, he is a lieutenant or captain in a police jurisdiction in the other state. This works best if you managed to figure out what type of cop you are dealing with and your imaginary brother just happens to be the same kind.(Sheriff, Trooper, etc.)

This little charade may be adjusted to fit your own particular set of circumstances. If you are in your fifties, the cop could be your son who just made it onto the force and you are so proud of him. If you are college age, the cop could be your new stepfather who just married your mother. Don't make him your daddy because, having grown up with a cop would make you more knowledgeable about police than most civilians really are. To the ladies out there, I wouldn't suggest that you claim he is your husband for the same reason, nor should the men claim their wife is the cop. A brother, uncle, or cousin should work fine.

Be sure to point out that your relative/policeman works in another state. Police officers are a close knit fraternity. If you claim that you are related to a cop in the same state, you might find out that the officer you are talking to was recently transferred from that area and knows all the cops who work there.

If you are uncomfortable with that one, then you might try the next best thing. Before starting on a trip, call up the State Police or Highway Patrol in the state where you will be traveling. Find out the name of the first or second in command. Let's assume that it is a gentleman named Assistant Deputy Superintendent William A. Bossman. If a member of that organization stops you, apologize for speeding and simply say, "Before you write that ticket, would it be possible for you to call Bill Bossman? This is very embarassing and I hate to impose on his friendship like this but I sure don't need a speeding ticket." (Be sure not to say you don't need "another" speeding ticket.)

The cop will want to know how you know his boss and under what circumstances. Yet, he will not want to appear to be prying about the personal life of his boss, so his questions will be limited. You will be vague and mention that, if you had your address book with you then you would have "Good Old Bill's home phone number." Notice, you use the familiar "Bill" rather than the title and formal name. Let's also be realistic. If you are driving a 1974 vintage car with terminal rust, no muffler and bald tires, is it likely you would know one of the highest ranking police officers in the state? If the cop starts pumping you for more information, just say, "Look, I've known him for a very long time. If you have to, just give me the ticket."

First, do you really think some lowly road cop is going to telephone his big boss to ask if you know him? Do you think the same lowly cop is going to take a chance on ticketing a close friend of some boss who may or may not be inclined to cost him a promotion in the future? It is a lot easier to just tell you to slow down and let you go. Be sure to tell him thank you.

There is a whole list of people who are often let

go with a warning. If you are one of those people, it is important to let the cop know it as soon as you can work it into the conversation. (Remember the thirty second rule?) Before going any further with tricks that have worked, perhaps it would help to give you the list. You might have an ace in the hole and not even know it. Here they are:

Firemen (professionals get more consideration than volunteers)
Ambulance and rescue workers
Prison guards
Doctors
Nurses
Priests, Ministers and Nuns

Let's now take a closer look at the last entry on the list. All the others are logical. They are, in a sense, kindred spirits, emergency workers. How is it that clergy so frequently get a break? Is it possible that we cops are just taking out a little insurance for the next life? I can't say. I can tell you that I have never known a priest, minister or nun to receive a ticket. With that in mind, let me tell you another little war story.

More than a decade ago, I chanced to notice a car, occupied by a lone woman, traveling at seventy-eight miles per hour. As I approached the car, the driver, a very pretty young lady, looked up and smiled. She wore a black skirt, below the knee, dark black nylons, black shoes, a white blouse and black sweater. The only jewelry was a large crucifix hanging around her lovely neck. Next to her, on the front seat was a wimple and veil with black bobby pins attached to it. Her hair was pinned in a pile on the top of her head. My first thought was a chauvinistic, "What a shame such a good-looking young woman is a nun." On the back seat was a Bible and some other religious books.

Before I had a chance to ask for her license and registration, she began telling me how sorry she was for speeding but she had to pick up two other "sisters" at the airport and they would be concerned if she was late. When I then asked for her paper work, she said her brother let her use his car while he was out of the country, "visiting the missions." I glanced at the last name on the registration and saw it matched the one on the nun's license. To be honest, I was more interested in looking at her date of birth to see how old she was.

I cautioned her to slow down and sent her on her way with a smile and a tip of the stetson. She very sweetly reached up and grasped my hand while saying, "Thank you and God bless you." As I got back in my troop car, she waved while pulling away. I sat in my patrol car and just felt uneasy about the stop. Something was not right. She was just too sure of herself and "polished." Nuns are generally very nervous when stopped. As I went about my duties, I just could not get that nun out of my mind.

About a week later at shift change, one of the troopers who had just completed his tour was talking about this beautiful nun he had caught speeding. "Naturally" he had let her go and he was quite impressed by her good looks. I asked what kind of car she was driving and it was soon apparent we had both pulled over the same person. As we compared notes, the other trooper even related how she had taken his hand and had said, "God bless you." He then mentioned that it surprised him that the church would permit a nun to have such long fingernails with bright red polish.

It hit me like a ton of bricks. We had both been conned! I then instantly realized what else had troubled me about the stop. She had been wearing perfume and although she was not wearing earrings, her ears had been pierced! I blurted out to a room full of troopers. . . . "That was no nun, that was a lady!" When the laughter finally died down, I told them of my suspicions. While talking about the "mystery nun," the other trooper remembered a decal on the back window that advertised a line of cosmetics. We both then remembered two suitcases on the floor of the back seat that looked like large sample cases.

It took me quite a while but I finally found her. Again she was speeding in excess of seventy. When I walked up to her, she didn't even recognize me and went into the exact same litany she had worked before with such success.

This time I paid more attention to her surroundings than her very attractive face and body. The "props" were in the same spots and she was again speeding to "pick up two sisters at the airport." The sample cases were on the floor behind the front seats and an opaque garment bag was hanging on the passenger side rear hook. There was also an appointment book laying under her wimple. Some music cassettes on the dashboard were from popular rock groups. A zippered make-up case could be seen peeking out of the top of her purse. I was sure that Sister Mary Sweetness was as bogus as they come.

I played along with her for a short while as she again told me all about her brother letting her have his car while he was off "visiting the missions." After asking her a few routine questions, I said, "How long have you been in sales?" Without thinking she blurted out, "About four years." It took a couple of seconds for her to realize what had happened and she then scrambled to try to cover the mistake by claiming she had misunderstood my question and had been a nun for four years. Nevertheless, the truth soon came out.

A check of her driver's license record revealed numerous speeding arrests yet, for the previous year, she had received no tickets of any kind. It turned out she was employed as a regional sales manager for a cosmetic firm and her job required that she be on the road almost all the time. She had been getting more than her share of speeding tickets and the Department of Motor Vehicles had sent her a notice that said she would lose her license if she got one more. Like many of us, she just couldn't bring herself to drive at the speed limit, so she devised her little plan out of desperation.

She told me how, after reaching a new city, she would check into her motel, change clothing and then make her planned rounds of meetings and appointments. She even proudly told me how she occasionally got a bonus. When arriving at one motel she had received a fifteen per cent reduction on her room because the desk clerk assumed she was clergy. The young woman was quick to point out to me that she had never actually claimed to be a nun and that I was the one who had made an improper assumption. When I pointed out she had lied about picking up two sisters at the airport, her response was, "I have two sisters and a brother. I might have been going to pick them up." My laughter showed her I was less than convinced.

After I gave her a much disserved ticket for speeding, she ended up almost begging me to tell her how I had known she was not a nun. I looked at her with my most professional frown and said "Police work m'am, just old-fashioned police work." Can you imagine the shock of seeing a girl dressed as a nun glare at you and say "Bullshit?" O. K. Ms. Sexy Nun, if you paid for this book, now you know. It was just your good looks and bad luck that caught you that time.

In reality, she did a great job at beating the system, even though I caught her. For a full year she had sped with impunity and never was ticketed. As a result, by the time she received a ticket from me enough points had been removed from her license so she could continue to drive. I bet she is still out there now, driving around with her Bible and black veil, tooling along at about seventy-five.

If I were a traveling salesman, the first items I would buy would be a roman collar and a black shirt. A few bumper stickers like "Jesus Saves" or "God is my Co-pilot" and in many cases, I wouldn't even be pulled over. How far a person might decide to maintain a charade would be entirely up to you but before you consider trying to assume the role of a cleric or anyone else, for that matter, it is important to talk to your lawyer. Each state will have their own statutes with respect to criminal impersonation and what would be perfectly legal in one state might get you arrested in another. If you are found out to be a fraud, the cop might not be amused.

You might also consider becoming a minister. It is my understanding that some "churches" sell certificates attesting to ordination as part of what appears to me to be a scheme to avoid taxes. I don't know any cop who ever took the trouble to find out to what church a priest or minister was affiliated with before letting him go. There is also a real neat bumper sticker that just says "CLERGY" that works very well.

A most important point is that you look like a member of the clergy. Your car should have a religious medallion on the dashboard and a Bible somewhere in plain view. Your car should not have any decals such as parking lot permits that would not be on a minister's car. Don't forget that the registration might be a give away if it is a company car. Have a reasonable explanation prepared in advance.

An identification card carried adjacent to your driver's license would be a good idea but do not present it to the cop. If he is anything but a rookie, he will be able to see it in your wallet. With that in mind, keep a separate wallet for all your business cards. With a little effort you can come up with a few of your own ideas. Good luck.

CHAPTER 5

Famous Last Words

At the risk of being redundant, I must again remind you that most people who get tickets have managed to talk themselves into them. By now I would hope that you have accepted the fact that it is possible and reasonable to expect to be stopped for speeding and to get away unscathed. With your new found positive attitude, let's explore some pitfalls that have adversely affected other motorists.

You have learned the stupidity of blustering "See you in Court" and now realize that, even what you say AFTER you get a ticket can still do you more harm than good. Please keep that in mind as you read this chapter because many of the "don'ts" are often uttered after the ticket is issued.

For starters, the first "don't" is: Don't sit there silent, like a bump on a log. Perhaps there is somewhere high in the Cascade Mountain Range of

Washington State, or deep in the Okefenokee Swamp of Georgia, a hermit who has never seen a television and does not know that he "has the right to remain silent." If you are driving on an interstate highway, then obviously that hermit is not you. If you sit there silent, the cop will label you as someone who is being silent to avoid self-incrimination. He will then make the assumption you will be pleading not guilty and he will react accordingly by issuing you a carefully written ticket with bunches of notes on his copy. I am not saying you have to incriminate yourself, but if you remain mute, the officer will perceive this as odd behavior and will be expecting an innocent plea. In addition, if you have said nothing, you have given the officer no reason to not give you a ticket.

How often has the officer been greeted with, "What's the problem?" Let's get serious folks. You know very well what the problem is. Your problem is you just got caught and the cop has the problem of putting up with you for a few minutes. If you are tooling along the interstate at a speed that will qualify for a ticket, you know why you are being stopped. Saying, "What's the problem?" should be avoided because it starts the conversation off with the insinuation that the officer is an irritant to you. That may be true but it neither feeds his ego nor reduces his fear by telling him. What is the cop thinking in response? "The problem is, I asked you for your license and registration, only to find you want to play twenty questions!"

In like manner the very lame question, "Was I speeding?" should never be used. I always wanted to respond with, "No, you were sitting still but your car was going like hell!" Do you suppose the motorist might become offended? This question, like the previous one insinuates you did not know you were speeding. I told you never to lie if the cop might know you are lying. Again, I would point out that in the cop's mind, if you are going fast enough to qualify for a ticket, then you must know you are speeding. Most cops permit 10 to 20 mph over the limit so they feel anyone going fast enough to get a ticket from them, was going so fast that they "had to know they were speeding." You might not realize exactly how fast you were going but you should know you were traveling in excess of the limit.

"I was just going with traffic." What a dumb comment to make to a cop who just finished chasing you! If you were going at the same speed that everyone else was going, then you just told the cop he is not doing his job because everyone else must have been speeding too. Even if this was true, would you intentionally tell a cop who is considering giving you a ticket, that he is not doing his job? In addition, if you really were "just going with traffic," he would not have singled you out. Before mouthing these foolish words, THINK! Have you recently passed any cars? Chances are the answer will be "yes." Then ask yourself, "Have vehicles been passing me?" and the answer will usually be "No." The cop also knows this and he knows you are lying to him. Even if he has not been following you, his radar will have told him the speed that traffic was going and your speed will have been above that for him to have singled you out. I have had drivers make this comment after being pulled over in the middle of the night when no other ''traffic'' was even in sight. The comment is deemed by the cop as argumentative. People who argue with cops always lose by getting tickets.

The next frequently used gem is, ''My speedometer is broken.'' It is heard so often that the officer just assumes you are lying. That is also not the impression you should be wanting to make with a cop who may be about to give you a ticket. In addition, it is no excuse and if you were seen to be passing other vehicles by the cop, he will only be irritated by that comment.

How many times has someone told me, ''I had my cruise control set at sixty-two,'' when they had been pulled over for seventy or more in a fifty-five zone! The sensation of speed at sixty-two is nothing like seventy and anyone driving a car who does not know the difference has no business on the road. They are also informing me it is O. K. to speed at certain rates and I should ignore them. Although true, why anger a cop by saying so. You will also appear to be a bit argumentative and, as said before, this should be avoided at all times.

''I'm sorry.'' Maybe, once during my career, I ran into a person who was truly contrite but I doubt it. What you really mean is, ''I'm sorry I was caught.'' Either way it hardly matters. Cops are not offended by most speeders and don't expect an apology. They just have to write a certain number of tickets so as to justify their existence and keep their bosses off their backs. Unless you have been going so fast that the policeman construes it as a personal affront to his integrity, he just doesn't care. Some of the cops do enjoy the challenge that goes into catching you but it doesn't matter to them whether you are sorry or not. It also sounds very phony! In addition, who, in their right mind, would not be feeling remorse at the prospect of getting a speeding ticket? Picture this: You look up at the officer and whine, "I'm sorry," and he smirks down at you while saying, "I know."

"I'm sorry," can sometimes be used to your advantage if you put it in conjunction with something else. If used by itself, it sounds like an adolescent who just got caught by mommy with daddy's dirty books. He knows he is in trouble and can think of nothing else to plead his case. Is this the impression you want to give the cop? If you use it with another comment like, "I'm sorry, but I think I left the coffee pot on and I won't feel right until I get home, etc." or "I'm sorry, but I'm late and if I miss this business appointment I will lose the account and get canned." You get the idea. If you use the words "I'm sorry" follow them with "but" and an excuse that indicates you didn't want to be speeding but had to anyway.

You could also use the words "I'm sorry," if you put it in conjunction with something like, "I'm sorry to have caused you this aggravation," or "I'm sorry to have caused you this trouble." Thus feeding the officer's ego.

Never, never use the words, "Do you know?" Somewhere, somehow, the public got the idea that if they were able to name enough police officers then the cop giving the ticket would change his mind. Mind you, I am not contradicting myself with respect to the "Not Guilty by Association" ploy in the last chapter. There is quite a big difference. In that part of the book, I explained how you might avoid a ticket by claiming to be related to a cop not known by the officer who stopped you. I also told how pretending to be good friends with a high ranking police officer might help you avoid a ticket. What I am referring to now is something completely different, where the violator (that's you, sport) believes if he can name cops who the officer knows then a ticket won't be written. The conversation might go something like this:

Officer: "License and registration please."

Violator: "Say, do you know Tpr. Jones?"

Officer: "No. Your license and reg. please."

Violator: "You MUST know Joe Jones. He's out of the Newport Barracks."

Officer: "No, I don't know him. About your license?"

Violator: "Well, if you don't know him, do you know Tpr. Smith. He's a real good friend of mine."

Officer: "No. I don't know him either."

Violator: "But you must. He's been on the force for about fifteen years."

Officer: "Nope."

Violator: "Then do you know Corporal Dowrite? He gave a talk on drugs at our club."

Officer: "No. Let's have your license and reg. Now!"

Violator: "You have to know Corporal Dowrite. Everybody knows Bob Dowrite."

Officer: "Listen, asshole. First, I said I never heard of him. Second, his name is Bill, not Bob, and third, if I don't have your license in my hand in thirty seconds, you're going to jail!"

Does anyone out there actually think that a police officer will let you go just because you manage to remember a cop's name? Those names have been on the radio, television, and in the newspapers every time a bad accident is investigated. It is simple to memorize a few cops names to use when stopped. It may be simple but it won't work.

When you stop to analyze it, there is no reason to expect it should work. As in every line of business, there are personality conflicts among the co-workers. How could you, the violator, possibly know if the officer that stopped you even likes the cop whose name you drop? When someone tried dropping cop names on me, no matter which cop name it was, I would put on my nastiest glare and say to the driver, "Yea, I know that officer. I know him real well. He cost me a promotion." That generally shut the man up quickly. I can honestly say that I never had a fellow trooper approach me later to ask what I had been talking about.

Another reason why this does not work is because

the officer who stops you has no way of knowing just how good a friend of the cop you are. If he was sure you were a good friend, even if he hated the other cop, he probably would let you off so as to avoid the hassle of being asked to get the ticket fixed, when your cop friend intercedes for you. Yet, so many people have claimed such close friendship with other officers that it is not uncommon for someone to ask us if we know ourselves? I have been present when it has happened to two different officers. Just don't ask, "Do you know. . . ." Too many others do it, too often.

If you are good friends with a cop, or lie very well, you can approach the "Do you know" concept in a manner that could be expected to work. It would be done something like this:

Officer: "License and registration please."

Violator: "Sure. Say, Joe Jones was over to the house just last week and was teasing my kid about getting a ticket. It's going to be very embarrassing when he hears about this. I think Joe is out of the Newport Barracks now, isn't he? My license is right here in my wallet."

It's obvious to even a retarded ape what you are trying to do, yet, done in this manner, it is more apt to get positive results. I should point out now that there is another time when you SHOULD use a cop's name. It is in conjunction with a "P.B.A." or other type of courtesy card. This will be explained in detail, in another part of the book.

"Officer, I promise not to speed anymore." While relaxing, comfortably reading this book, most of you would find it hard to believe anyone might say this to a cop but it happens with shocking regularity. Perhaps in the fear and panic some people experience when being stopped by a cop, they regress to being childlike. "Please mommy, don't punish me. I promise to be good."

Just look how far you have progressed already. You now should know why this comment is of no use without my even having to tell you! At the risk of losing that small minority who find reading comprehension difficult, and because you are paying for it anyway, I will be redundant.

Oh, good grief! It looks like I just did it again! Sorry folks, I just can't resist occasionally insulting the reader. After all those years abusing the public, it's not easy to rein in my dripping sarcasm. At any rate, I digress. It's time to educate you some more.

Promising not to speed anymore will do you no good because the cop does not care if you continue to speed or not. What would be your reaction if the police told you, "If you plead guilty, I promise not to ticket anybody else for speeding." It would be a worthless promise to make because you don't care if someone else gets caught speeding. In like manner, the cop doesn't care if you continue to speed.

This next one may anger many of you but sometimes the truth hurts. Don't point out to the nice uniformed gentleman, "I fought for my country. I'm a vet!" and expect him to fall on his knees while begging you to forgive him for being so unreasonable as to stop you. There are quite a few variations of this, such as, "I fought in the big one, WW 2," or "I was wounded while fighting for this country." We also got plenty of, "I spent a year risking my life in Vietnam, when my country called." I ask you, just what does entering the military have to do with speeding?

Before all the veteran blood out there reaches a boiling point, let me explain. In spite of what you just read, I am a veteran of the Vietnam era myself and am very proud of it but this chapter is not about the respect due to veterans. It has to do with what NOT to say to a cop. Because of the reasons I will soon explain, it is not a good idea to expect to be let out of a ticket by so vocally claiming your veteran status.

Let's look at what makes up the police agencies in this country. During the Vietnam era, police recruits were drawn almost exclusively from the ranks of young veterans. Many of them had combat records that few soldiers could equal. These men had first promised to risk their life for their country and then returned to the U.S.A. only to subsequently promise to again risk that life to protect others, as a police officer. Most of them resented driver's insinuating it was unpatriotic to ticket someone just because the violator was also a veteran.

It is also an interesting point but one learned from fellow officers who were combat veterans. The men who saw the most action, were the ones who would do their best to avoid talking about the subject. Is it not reasonable to then assume that someone who is so quick to demand special consideration by claiming to be a veteran, probably never did anything heroic? If they had been in the thick of combat, they would avoid talking about it and wouldn't bring it up so easily.

When the pool of Vietnam era veterans began to get too old for entering police work, agencies vainly attempted to replace the maturity those vets had brought to the job, with education. Degrees with names like ''Police Science'' or ''Criminal Justice'' began to appear. With those degrees came young men and women with college but virtually no military experience. They don't like you reminding them that they chose not to serve their country and most of them neither appreciate nor understand what it means to be a veteran. They see your claims to be argumentative and overbearing.

To best take advantage of the police officers who would tend to give preference to a veteran, without angering those who are not so inclined, I would suggest you invest in a small decal and place it on your driver's side rear window. No cop worth his salt would miss seeing the decal and your silence on the subject would tend to achieve the results you may have thought you would get by ''sounding off.'' A small metal crest or shield proclaiming your veteran status, attached to your rear bumper would also say much more than words.

Because most of you assume you will be getting the ticket, and because human nature causes us to never want to admit when we are wrong, many of the ''no no'' comments are uttered in anger. They serve no legitimate purpose and cause the officer to instantly decide a ticket is warranted. Here are a few of the most common examples:

"I want to see the radar display." Believe it or not, there are people out there who are so foolish as to actually make such a demand on a cop. If you analyze it, this is a brainless, futile gesture. Most states have no statute requiring that the officer show the violator anything except the ticket. Even if such a statute exists in your state, just what do you think such actions will accomplish? I have news for you. The cop can make the radar display "lock on" to any speed he desires and even if the unit is reading "OO," does anyone think, after acting like such a pompous fool, the cop will let the man off? If the violator thinks he is building his case for court then he should also remember the last thing someone should want the cop to know is that the violator would ever consider going to trial. Be smart and forget about the radar display. Asking to see it can get you a ticket when none was going to be written.

"What is your name?" We can link this with the similar dumb question, "What is your badge number." Now think, folks, will his giving you this information aid you in any way? Will this reduce the officer's fear or build his ego? About the only things it will build is his blood pressure and your insurance premiums. My insulting response was always a smile and a friendly, "It's on the bottom of the ticket."

Then there's the "You're a cop so you must be a racist" accusation. It always starts out with the line, "You just stopped me because I'm————." In the blank space, the reader can feel free to insert the racial designation of his choice, except white.

The most common ones are Black, Indian and Hispanic. Rest assured, the cop has heard all of them.

It is amazing! The police car is closing on the violator at a combined speed of 140 mph. The radar goes off and he looks across the median to see a speeding car, with tinted glass. As often as not, it is also in the middle of the night. He finally gets the car pulled over, walks up to the driver's door and hears an angry, accusing voice from inside the car saying, "You just stopped me because I'm black!" Give the poor cop a break! Only Superman has X-ray vision and that radar unit on the dash just registers speed. If you're a young black man, the next time you get stopped, tell the cop, "You just stopped me because I was speeding!" It should work. It's hard for a cop to write a ticket while he's laughing so hard he can't breathe. To be serious, is there a member of a minority anywhere who believes a cop will refrain from writing a ticket, after he has just been accused of racism?

Make no mistake about it. In police work, racism not only exists but is practiced by many officers, both white and minority. It has been my experience that most white cops are less inclined to give a minority a break and most minority cops are more inclined to ticket a white while letting the minority go. I know of no municipality that keeps statistics to prove me right or wrong. I doubt the heads of most agencies want to acknowledge there is a problem, but there is. Let's assume the reader is a minority and has just been pulled over by a "racist" cop. Your chances of avoiding a ticket are LESS but if you confront the cop, accusing him of racism, your chances of then avoiding the ticket no longer exist at all! The cop may or may not be a racist but if you accuse him of being one, then you are guaranteed a ticket. You also manage to alienate any officer who is not a racist, by falsely accusing him. If you think about it, when a minority accuses a cop of pulling him over due to racism, that minority is himself, making a racist assumption and statement. Who among us is entitled to "cast the first stone?"

Do cops in your area practice racism? Judge for yourself. Just purchase a police scanner, put it in your home and keep track of the percentage of computer checks done on minorities. Also, when you hear one cop tell another that a certain vehicle is a "good check," rest assured they are not referring to a well-behaved tourist from Czechoslovakia!

One more gem guaranteed to give you a ticket is to claim you were not speeding. Never directly contradict what a cop says. When the cop says he stopped you for speeding, he does not want to hear, "No I wasn't!" or "I was NOT speeding!" Let's not forget the standard police personality. How dare you call that cop a liar!!! Who do you think you are telling him he may have made a mistake!! It's better to give a reason why your attention would have been elsewhere. Want an example? "Officer, I had no idea my speed had creeped up so high. It's been a long trip and my attention was on the guy in front of me. I think he was falling asleep. Thank you for bringing it to my attention." Does it sound like you are sucking up to the guy? Of course it does. Even he will realize it but feed his ego while reducing the fear.

Here's a good one. Often the officer will try to set you up by asking you, "Do you know how fast you were going?" That's like the old question, "Have you stopped beating your wife yet?" No matter what you say, you dig a bigger hole. If you say you were driving at the speed limit, you are considered a liar by the cop and in his mind, you will deserve the ticket. If you are truthful, he can point out later in court that you admitted speeding. Sometimes the cop will be uncertain as to whether he has stopped the correct car. By asking you that question, if you are honest, the officer can confirm to himself that he stopped the correct vehicle.

How can you possibly side step this attack? It's hard to say. It depends on the cop. Your best bet is to try a comment like, "I just wasn't paying attention like I should have officer, how fast was I going?" You put the ball back in his court. When he tells you your speed, act surprised and respond with something like, "I had no idea!" If he is not sure your car was the one clocked, he will let you go. If he is sure, he will be inclined to think of you as a nice guy. (A little stupid perhaps but what do you care what he thinks of you?) The important thing is you have admitted nothing and given him no reason to be insulted. For those of you who would be inclined to say something like, "No way! I couldn't have been going that fast." I suggest you read the last few paragraphs over again.

Last but not least, let us address the few ladies who are still out there that look up at the cop through their fluttering eyelashes and with tongue wetting their lips, use the old line, ''I'll do anything to avoid a ticket.'' Often included in the show are open buttons on the blouse and a skirt hiked up nearly to the panty line. Give the cop a break! If you are that easy, what cop in his right mind would want to take a chance on getting a disease? In the last few years, these ladies have become scarce. I must admit, if the women's rights movement has accomplished nothing else, at least it has cut down on the number of women with no self-respect. (Either that or the fifty pounds I gained changed their attitude toward me. I'm not sure which. . . .)

CHAPTER 6

After The Ball Is Over

Before reading this book, most of you thought a ticket was inevitable if you were stopped. In this chapter, let's assume what you always expected has happened. The cop just told you, "You're getting a ticket." O.K., you can't win them all. Nevertheless, it is in your best interest to cut your losses. As was explained in an earlier chapter, what you do both before and after the ticket is written, may have a direct bearing on your lawyer's ability to get you off with the traditional slap on the wrist. Even if you choose not to fight the charge, your attitude might very well affect how much the ticket will cost you, especially in states that do not have preset fines for violations.

Most importantly, when the cop tells you he is going to issue you a summons, make no assumption it is written until it is in your hot little hand. Don't stop trying to have him change his mind just because he told you a ticket would be issued. A good response would be, "I really wish you would reconsider because. . . ."

Now is the time to really plea bargain. Tell him flat out that you can't afford to get a costly speeding ticket. Give the reasons why, and ask him to consider writing you a ticket for a lesser offense, such as an equipment violation. The reasons for your request could be anything from pleading poverty, to the prospect of your losing your job. There also could be a combination of reasons. Just make them realistic. Even if you are driving a luxury car you can claim that, without your driver's license, you won't be able to continue to work. Your attitude should be that of a contrite person asking the cop to be kind to you. Make him want to do you a favor.

Don't adopt a tone or posture that would indicate your problems will be his fault if he writes the ticket. Comments like, "Well there goes my job. I might as well go on welfare." or "You're putting my family on welfare," should be avoided. This will be resented by the cop as he knows HE wasn't the one who was speeding.

Keep in mind, for all you know, the ticket might just be a warning and a suddenly surly attitude coupled with a smart mouth could get you the real McCoy issued in a hurry. Now is not the time to deviate from the program this book is trying to teach you. Just continue to feed the officer's ego while reducing any residual fear.

You know that you should not demand to know his name. Why make any demands on him at all?

You should also not try to read his name on his uniform. Most cops will notice what you are doing and will take offense to this. When he hands you the ticket, it is normal procedure for him to explain how to answer the summons. Before he begins, interrupt him if you have to and ask, "Can I plead guilty by mail?" Look directly into his face at the same time, with a contrite expression. You will then be accomplishing a number of things at one time. As soon as you mention pleading guilty by mail, the cop will begin the process of lumping you together with thousands of other forgotten times and faces. Oh what a great place in his mind for you to be! In addition, you will be in the process of forming any testimony you may end up giving at a trial. Read on!

Attempt to memorize all of the facial characteristics that you can and at the same time say "Thank you." I know it seems like a stupid thing to say but when the District Attorney calls him to ask if you gave him any trouble, that "Thank you" could be worth a lot of money in your pocket.

What color hair does he have? Is there any facial hair? Is his nose broken or are there any scars? How are his teeth? Why should you try to memorize his description? If you go to court, it is possible that a different officer will show up, claiming to have written the ticket. If you can testify that he is not the cop who ticketed you, and can show notes you have written, describing the "other cop" differently, it could create some doubt in the mind of the judge. There are a number of reasons why this might happen, none of them honest. They have to do with a few cops not writing enough tickets and other, more aggressive cops (usually rookies) "helping them out." Nobody said all cops were honest and a few older cops aren't above coercing a young officer into doing their work for them.

For those of you who think that last paragraph was "far-fetched." I can assure you, worse things have been perpetuated by cops who were lazy or were pushed too hard by supervisors. More than a few recently deceased people have been issued a ticket while they were lying peacefully in their graves. The name and date of birth of the deceased, are listed on the marker. That, and information available in the state's Motor Vehicle Dept. computer, are all a cop needs to write a back dated ticket.

You should take plenty of notes if you are planning on pleading not guilty or if you anticipate turning the ticket over to your lawyer. It is just as important that you refrain from taking those notes until you and the officer have parted company. It is best to wait until you drive away and stop elsewhere to take these notes. Don't just pull over on the side of the road or the cop is certain to pass you and notice. Use a rest area or exit. Don't sit there waiting for the cop to leave. He should wait until you have pulled out.

I remember a businessman who I had stopped for speeding. He was a fairly decent guy, just trying to make a living and I had decided I would probably let him go with a warning. I advised him I would "be with him shortly" and returned to my patrol car to check his driver's license on the computer.

As I waited for the computer response, he began scribbling notes on a pad. When I returned to his car, he had the nerve to begin asking me questions as to exactly where I had caught him and how far I had clocked him. HOW DARE THIS MERE MORTAL QUESTION MY VERACITY! Could it be possible he would actually think that I, Mr. Good Guy Incarnate, could possibly err!!?? Ladies and gentlemen, those last two sentences give you a fine example of the police mentality. The police ego must never be even slightly wounded by the violator. This man probably did not even realize he was acting in an insulting manner. He got his ticket and, would you believe, mailed in a guilty plea! Had it not been for his note taking and foolish questions, he would have driven away with a smile on his face. It is important for you to take notes so as to help your attorney, just be sure you drive to the next exit or rest area before doing so.

Before you pull out, note the odometer of your car so you can testify later to exactly where you were stopped. By checking again at the next exit, you will be able to testify you were pulled over "exactly two and three tenths of a mile east of the Main Street exit." Judges are impressed by thoroughness. If you can do it without being too obvious, jot down the plate number of the police car. If he had clocked you and brings the speedometer certification of another car, you should win the case. Also note the road and weather conditions, along with the exact time and traffic conditions.

Last, but not least, even if your intention is to just pay the ticket and forget it, don't ask to pay the fine to the officer. In some states, this is common practice but in other states it might be construed as a veiled attempt to offer the cop a bribe. If you are just planning to plead guilty, you should prefer to send in your plea directly to the judge because he also has the option of reducing the charges. You can always enclose a letter pointing out any mitigating circumstances or reasons why he should be lenient. If you choose to do this, be sure to mention in the letter how courteous and professional the cop was, even if he acted like a blood-crazed Nazi. Often the judge will ask the officer what happened and what was your "attitude." The judge may also let the cop read your letter before deciding to reduce the charges. I even have copies of some of the more humorous letters judges have received. Is it not reasonable, now that you know this, to mention in your letter what a "great guy" the officer was?

CHAPTER 7

How Radar Really Works
& Other Cop Toys

(Subtitle—How the 60 mph tree
made history)

This is the big one! Here is the chapter many of you probably turn to first and the one that will be the basis on which I believe the whole book will often be judged. I assure you I am acutely aware of how important this information is to you in your efforts to avoid getting caught. Explaining a technical subject is never easy. I have tried my best to keep it simple. To those who find this chapter a little like reading their first grade primer, I apologize and urge you to keep in mind, the information contained herein is none the less valuable.

To understand the modern radar used by traffic

cops, it is a big help to also understand how the radar unit evolved. Let us then begin with a little bit of a history lesson on speed enforcement.

The term RADAR is an acronym derived from "RAdio Detection And Ranging." Some primitive studies and theories involving the concept of radar can be found in the late 1800s yet most of the discoveries and inventions resulting in the modern traffic radar, were a result of research during World War II. The ability to see ships and aircraft at night or beyond the distance of normal eyesight became imperative.

All radar works in basically the same way. First you need a transmitter that will send out a series of electromagnetic waves. These waves, which we will also refer to as a "beam," travel at about the speed of light and are invisible. To help illustrate traffic radar, we will draw a parallel to a simple flashlight. The transmitter is the lightbulb and batteries. When turned on, the flashlight starts producing a beam of light.

Once the energy is produced by the transmitter, it is sent in a specific direction by the radar antenna. This antenna actually serves two or more functions but for now let's ignore the others and just view it as the device that makes the radar beam directional. Were it not for the antenna doing this, the waves produced by the transmitter would be going in all directions like the waves on a pond when you throw in a stone or like the radar an air traffic controller uses that looks in a complete circle. The lens and polished surface surrounding the bulb on your flashlight does the same thing as the police radar antenna.

Without their help, the light generated by the bulb would just diffuse in all directions. With their help, a beam of light is created which you can point at any item you desire to illuminate. The antenna on the radar unit works exactly the same way, sending out a beam that can be directed at a specific direction or item (your car).

Now that we have a tool that can send out a beam and we have modified that tool so we are able to send that beam in a specific direction, let's tape a simple light meter to the flashlight. Any light that is reflected back toward the flashlight will be measured by the light meter.

Take your flashlight into a darkened room, turn it on and point it at a large mirror on the wall. The light meter will register a higher reading as the beam of light is reflected from the mirror back toward the flashlight. Just as the light meter picks up the reflected beam of light from the mirror, the antenna on the radar unit picks up the reflected electromagnetic waves that bounce off the front of your car. As you get closer to the radar unit, each individual wave that strikes the front of your car takes just a microsecond less time to get back to the antenna. The radar unit then measures the difference and computes your speed.

Conversely, if you are driving away from the radar source, each reflected wave that bounces off the back of your car will take a microsecond longer to reach the antenna, resulting in the unit being able to determine your speed by measuring this change. The faster you are going, the further each wave will have to travel and the longer it will take to return to the antenna.

Now stand at an angle to the mirror and again point your flashlight at it. What happens? Your spouse wakes up and threatens to have you committed to a mental institution if you don't stop playing and come to bed! Before you quickly turn off the flashlight and climb between the sheets, you should notice that the beam of light was reflected onto the opposite wall. By moving the flashlight, you would be able to make the beam illuminate any point on the wall that you desired while still pointing it at your mirror. Your light meter would then register much lower because the light was not being reflected back to it.

As soon as your spouse is again snoring, very quietly slide out of bed and go wake up junior. It will be necessary to enlist his aid in the next step of our physics experiment. Have him bring a small hand-held mirror and stand, with his back against the wall, where your beam of light had struck before. If you stand in exactly the same spot where you were earlier and again shine your flashlight at the large mirror, the light should reflect toward junior. If junior is able to hold his hand mirror so the reflected beam of light strikes it, he will be able to make the beam reflect again and shine elsewhere by moving his hand-held mirror. You should caution him in advance, not to let the ray of light fall upon the face of your snoring spouse or you may both end up using the flashlight to find the dog house.

When junior has had his fill of bouncing the light

all over your bedroom, have him hold his mirror so it directly faces the point where the flashlight beam is bouncing off the big mirror. The beam of light generated by your flashlight will now be leaving the flashlight, reflect off the big mirror, strike the small mirror held by junior, and bounce directly back again. As it continues its journey it should again hit the large mirror in the same spot and reflect back toward the flashlight. Your light meter will now register an increase as the light has been bounced back to you.

That was fun wasn't it? It is truly amazing the crazy things I can motivate people to do in the hopes of avoiding a ticket. Surprise! You have just solved the mystery of the 60 mph tree! Radar beams are subject to bouncing or reflecting off large items in the same way your flashlight beam bounced off your mirror. After reflecting off a large item such as a leafy maple tree or the side of a barn, they can then strike a vehicle and return via the same route from which they came until they again reach the antenna. The radar unit will measure the speed of the car, even though it is pointed at the maple tree or barn because the electromagnetic waves will reflect off the immobile item, strike the car and return to the radar unit by the same route.

A radar unit is an extremely accurate and dependable device for recording a vehicle's speed. It is, however only a tool and, like any tool, is only as competent as the person using it. The electronics industry, which makes and sells both radar and radar detectors, takes an active part in educating and certifying radar operators so they understand what false readings are and what causes them. At the same time, in order to boost the sale of radar detectors, they attempt to make their own reliable products (radar units) look unreliable to the public by pointing out the possibility of a unit being aimed at an inanimate object while the radar unit indicates a speed.

In the 1950s and early 1960s, radar units required considerable work to set up. As a result there were very few of them around and they were operated by "specialists." The antenna would be attached to a tripod that would be set on the edge of the road and a cable would then run from the antenna to the inside of the patrol car. Inside the car would be the transmitter and a readout unit that resembled a voltmeter. The officer had to watch the face of the readout as the needle climbed up the scale from zero each time a car drove past.

Because of the cable attachment to the antenna on the tripod, it required other officers to wait down the road until the radar operator called out the violator to them. You can see that this could result in mistakes being made as two similar cars came through at the same time. It also tied up the radio with chatter on a busy day.

To encourage officers to take undesirable special assignments, the most common carrot dangled before their noses is to offer them the possibility of becoming detectives or relieve them from having to work nights. Who, in their right mind, would want to sit in a police car day after day, with eyes glued to a radar readout? As a result, the radar detail in most jurisdictions became a day job, resulting in no radar being run at night. It caught lots of drivers during the day and the police hierarchy was happy.

About the same time that Vietnam was at its worst, the electronics industry introduced the hand-held radar unit, consisting of a bulky gun-shaped item containing transmitter, antenna and an electronic readout. It could be operated by an officer with a minimum of training at any time of the day or night. After using the radar unit on a speeder, the officer squeezed a trigger to record the speed, and then chased down his victim.

With the money pouring into the electronics industry for research and development of military hardware, is it any wonder that the electronics industry then was able to introduce something called "moving radar?" Prior to this introduction, radar could only be used if the operator was sitting still. Now, every time a cop was coming toward you, there was a chance he was "taking your picture."

The public no longer felt safe on our highways and demanded action. Our electronics industry perceived a demand to be filled and the result was massive sales of the citizen's band radio. Truckers began to group together in convoys and nearly everyone who traveled the interstate highway system became a "smokey reporter." Not to be outdone, the police armed themselves with the same citizen's band radios and the number of speeders being caught continued to spiral.

As sales of CB radios began to drop, the electronics industry needed a new darling to excite both the public and their stockholders. Here enters the radar detector. Because all police radar utilized the same frequencies, known as X-band, it was fairly simple to manufacture an item that would detect the presence of those particular electromagnetic radio waves. Citizens now had an early warning system capable of protecting them from the radar cop, but not for long.

Police agencies, now aware of the massive amount of money that could be made by radar use, demanded that the electronics industry "do something." Would any of us doubt they would? They simply introduced the K-band radar units. These units operated in the same manner as their predecessors but transmitted at a different wavelength so the radar detectors were unable to detect them. In doing this, the industry created a new demand for another new product.

You guessed it! Soon a radar detector was introduced which could detect both -X-band and K-band radars. We were back to square one but the electronics industry was never healthier. Although other speed enforcement devices were then placed on the market, nothing so adversely affected speeders or tipped the scales in the cop's favor like the simple invention of the instant on/off button.

Prior to the invention of the instant on/off button, radar units were turned on at the beginning of the shift and often were not turned off until the end of the shift. The car constantly produced electromagnetic radiation that could be detected by radar detectors long before the patrol car even came into view. The instant on/off feature keeps the transmitter warmed up and ready to go at all times but prevents the antenna from sending out a signal. With no signal being sent out, the speeder's radar detector would not have a signal to detect and so it would not sound an alarm.

I have heard owners of the more expensive radar detectors claim their units were capable of alerting on the active transmitter even if the cop's instant on/off button kept the radar antenna from activating, yet when field tested by me, using a police radar unit, they didn't even activate when the patrol car containing the radar unit was parked directly beside the car equipped with the detector.

With all the publicity over the stealth bomber, it was unavoidable that someone would try to market some type of "stealth" item for cars. The latest item I have heard about is a shroud that fits the nose of the car. I have yet to find anything that works. You should know that even a stealth bomber is visible to radar that is activated from above and, if going down the runway, it would be able to be "clocked" with police radar. Years ago people claimed that putting tinfoil in their hubcaps would work fine but nothing is going to stop those rays from bouncing off the car's surface, back to the antenna.

So how do you avoid getting caught by radar? You must learn a whole new way of interstate driving. To do it right, you will need a citizens band radio and a radar detector. Once more I will exercise my amazing psychic powers and attempt to delve into the reader's mind. You are thinking "Didn't he just point out that radar detectors are no good?" The answer to that question is an emphatic "NO!" The instant on/off switch on the officer's radar unit greatly diminishes a detectors capability yet it is still the best game in town, IF YOU UNDERSTAND WHAT THE UNIT IS TELLING YOU! Before we begin to teach you this new way of driving, it will be necessary for you to learn a few more things.

I would hope that my explanation of the basic police radar unit, using your flashlight as an example, gave you a better understanding of the radar concept. Now that you have that understanding, it will be necessary to teach you how "moving radar" works.

To begin with, you will remember that the radar sent out an invisible beam of electromagnetic pulses. To best explain how moving radar works, try to picture two separate radar beams. In the interest of simplicity, we will call them beam "A" and beam "B." Although they are two separate beams, they both are generated by the same transmitter and are directed out the front of the patrol car by the same antenna as the cop is driving down the road. Although they have the same transmitter and antenna, it would help if you thought of them as being transmitted on different frequencies. As a result, when they bounce back off different items and are received simultaneously by the antenna, that antenna can tell which electromagnetic pulses are from beam "A" and which originated from beam "B."

Have you ever noticed that some flashlights send out a light beam that gets wider quickly but weakens while other flashlights send out a thin beam that seems much brighter and does not widen perceptively? Well, picture the two radar beams doing the same thing. Radar beam "A" is a thin beam designed to bounce off the violator's car. It will measure the closing speed between the violator and the patrol car. If the patrol car is going 60 mph and the violator is going 75 mph, beam "A" will return, indicating a speed of 135 mph, the sum of both car's speeds.

While this is happening, beam "B" is also doing its job. It is opening wide and bouncing back from all kinds of stationary objects such as signs, delineators, trees, poles, bushes and guiderails. Because these items are stationary and the police car is closing on them at 60 mph, beam "B" reports the patrol car's speed of 60 mph to the radar unit.

The moving radar displays its results on a small console that usually sits on the police car's dashboard. It has two display ports labeled "patrol" and "violator." I am sure you have figured out that the results of beam "B" are displayed in the port labeled "patrol." If everything is working properly, this speed should be the same speed as is indicated by the speedometer of the patrol car. Understand that, very often, everything does not work properly.

While the 60 mph is being displayed in the "patrol" port, the radar unit is also subtracting that speed from the speed registered by beam "A." In our example, it would be subtracting 60 (Beam B) from 135 (Beam A). The result is displayed in the "violator" port and, of course, is the speed of the car being clocked. In this wonderful world of instant electronics, this is all done, and the results made available to the officer at a speed so fast that when your radar detector activates, you will not have time to take your foot completely off the accelerator. In fact, as you raise your foot, each mph that your car drops will register on the moving radar unit until the two cars have passed each other and your car is out of the beam.

In addition, beam "A" also is designed to emit a tone from the console. The faster the speed being measured, the higher pitched the tone becomes. The tone is heard even before the unit is able to compute and display the violator's exact speed. As a result, unless the cop is tone deaf, he knows by the sound that he is about to have a "good" readout.

It would seem that the odds are stacked against you so bad that you might as well give up and start obeying the speed limit. Perish the thought! Very often, the moving radar unit does not give an accurate speed and the cop knows it. This is one of the reasons the tone is so important. If the tone indicates a pitch that the officer has heard when cars have registered at 65 mph and he gets a reading at 80 mph, he should be trained well enough to know he should not pursue and ticket that car. Let me explain a couple of ways that the moving radar unit screws up.

Let's again go out on patrol with Officer Neckvein. He has placed his daily ration of cigars in the visor, safely stored his economy size bottle of antacid in the glove box, put one of each in his mouth and is ready to patrol. Good old Officer Neckvein wasn't born yesterday. In fact, he has been progressively growing out of his uniforms for over twenty years. He has never been promoted and now has seniority over all those young hotshot college kids that the Chief has been hiring as new patrolmen. As a result of his exulted position, he was able to pull rank on the other officers and is getting first crack at the new "moving radar" unit.

All the officers had recently been required to attend a refresher course on radar and these new units were covered. After all his time on the job the last thing Neckvein needed was to go over the basics of radar. Hell! He had been papering jokers using radar before some of the younger cops had even been a glint in their father's eye! Nobody is going to tell him about radar! Neckvein had spent the day in class, paging through a men's magazine and the instructor, another young cop, was not about to say anything to him.

As Neckvein opened the carrying case that contained the new unit, the first thing he pulled out was the antenna. It was a lot smaller than the old horn shaped ones that had to be mounted on the outside of the car's window. This one sat right on the dash. He then pulled out the console, containing the transmitter. The front was an array of knobs and buttons. They were all marked so this should be easy enough to figure out. He plugged in the power cord to the cigarette lighter and the unit lit up with the letters H O L D displayed in the ports.

Neckvein vaguely remembered the instructor mention something about the new units testing themselves. The machine said "H O L D" so that's what he did. He sat there holding the transmitter, waiting for it to tell him what to do next. As he glanced down at the carrying case, he saw the hold button and cord. A closer look at the unit showed where it plugged in. Trying to appear as casual as possible, he looked around and breathed a sigh of relief once he was sure no one had taken notice of him. He then set the transmitter/console on the dash, next to the antenna.

It took him a few more minutes to figure out how the clamps and suction cup devices secured the items to his dash but he managed without looking at the instructions. It was now getting to be a matter of principle. No way was he going to read that instruction booklet.

All this effort and aggravation had Officer Neckvein puffing just a little and the windshield began to fog over. As he thought to himself, "I guess I got to get back on that damn diet," he turned the car's defroster on high. His jaw suddenly went agape, causing the lit cigar to fall between his legs, as the radar unit displayed 18 mph.

After hastily retrieving his cigar, and wincing in pain as he slapped out the sparks, he tentatively reached for the defroster button and lowered it one notch. The unit then read 12 mph. His first thought was "Great! I wonder if it will self-destruct if I turn on the air conditioner! He assumed the unit had some kind of malfunction but he wasn't going to tell the Chief. The last time someone broke one of the radar units, the boss had a fit. He would just not use the defroster or air conditioner all day.

What had happened was quite simple to understand. The radar unit, having no other target, had measured the speed of the heater/defroster fan. It was going to be a long day for Neckvein. He next pushed a button marked "L.TEST" and both ports started flashing with zeros. He smugly congratulated himself for figuring out how to test the darn thing without laboring through all those pages in the user's manual.

One thing puzzled him. Every other radar unit he had ever used, always came with tuning forks. He was expected to strike the tuning forks and hold them up in front of the antenna to test the unit, before going on patrol. The forks would vibrate at a set speed and the unit would read out at that speed if working properly. This moving radar unit also came with tuning forks. He wondered why, if all you had to do was push a little button to test the unit. If he had read the instructions, he would have known the "L.TEST" button only tested the lights in the digital readouts of the ports. It didn't matter that much. Like most cops, he hadn't bothered to test the radar unit with tuning forks in years.

He was now ready to go out on the prowl. All the older radar units had lost some of their "zip" and would sometimes fail to give a read out. As a unit ages, it is not uncommon for it's range to become less. He was anxious to try out the abilities of this new one. When he activated the unit by releasing the hold button, he enjoyed seeing his speed read out in the "patrol" portal. It would be easier to use, than looking down at the speedometer so he often left the hold button disengaged, telling everyone with a radar detector, he was near.

Traffic was a little on the heavy side and quite a few of the big rigs were on the road. His first victim was a small red sports car that was passing one of the trucks. He pressed his hold button and the unit gave a readout of 45 mph as the sports car zipped past him at a speed closer to eighty than the forty-five. What had happened was obvious to even Neckvein's feeble mind. The radar had selected the truck as the target because it was a much larger mass of metal. Neckvein's first lesson was "You can't always get the target you want." The red sports car continued on unscathed.

A short time later, Neckvein sighted another likely target. This time his cruiser was climbing a hill, overtaking a truck when the speeder was seen approaching. Through clenched teeth, Neckvein snarled to himself, "No other car approaching in sight . . . you're mine, sucker." Neckvein tended to talk to himself quite a bit.

He estimated the violator to be traveling down the hill at about 70 to 75 mph. When the violator was fairly close, he deactivated the hold button and all hell broke loose. The radar unit started beeping and the "violator" port commenced to flash a speed of 102 mph. Neckvein was delighted as he looked for the nearest U-turn. "This moving radar is allllll righttttt."

Neckvein caught the man, wrote the ticket, and again went on patrol, chuckling to himself. "Boy was that driver mad! I almost got to punch him." He tried the moving radar a few more times and was quite satisfied with the results. He had been surprised at the high reading on the first car he had ticketed as the car didn't look like it was going that fast but, since then, the unit had been working splendidly and so he did not concern himself further.

By early afternoon, traffic was lighter and Neck-vein needed to put some miles on his odometer so his Chief would think he had been properly covering his post. He put his car in the passing lane, turned on the headlights and mashed the accelerator. Once his speedometer climbed past 95 mph he relaxed, concentrating on the traffic far ahead. That was when he first saw it. With traffic so light, a trucker had decided to take his chances while pulling an empty trailer and had also planted his accelerator to the floor. As the two vehicles approached, Neck-vein's face broke into a huge smile as he chanted to himself, "Gotcha gotcha gotcha gotcha gotcha." No other vehicles were in sight.

The trucker had also seen Neckvein's patrol car but was wise enough to know his rig would jack-knife if he tried to slow down too quickly. His truck was going well over 100 mph when his radar detector went off. He thought he could see his driver's license flying away on little silver wings, yet, fearing an accident, he dared not even pump the brakes.

Back in Neckvein's patrol car, the tension was almost visible as the vehicles closed on each other. With his foot still mashed on the patrol car's accelerator, and still chanting "gotcha gotcha gotcha gotcha gotcha," Neckvein pushed the hold button down and was rewarded with the highest pitched whistle he had ever heard. He triumphantly glanced at the "violator" portal on the console as the vehicles blasted by each other, and was rewarded with a readout of 00 mph. His jaw again went slack. His lit cigar again spiraled to his lap but Neckvein never noticed as the realization of what had not happened struck home. He had missed the truck! A chance that may come just once in a career was blown! The big one got away! He instinctly knew he would never get another chance like this. Catching a big rig going that fast was as rare as a virgin in a singles bar. Somehow he had blown it.

Lesson number two for Officer Neckvein. . . . "Moving radar often doesn't work if the patrol car is going at high speed." As Neckvein reached for the bottle of antacids a small column of smoke began curling past his mirrored sunglasses as the memory of his stogy was graphically brought home. He was not having fun today!

As his tour was close to its end, Officer Neckvein halfheartedly engaged the hold button and headed back to his station. As he was about to take his exit, he noticed one more car coming toward him. He again estimated the speed of the violator at about 68 mph. Just like his first ticket of the day, he was overtaking a slower moving truck. As he deactivated the hold button, he was shocked to again see a speed in excess of 100 mph. He mused "This is impossible! Could this damn machine be giving me that truck's speed now?? A lot of good that will do me!" Then he noticed something else strange. The speed registering in the patrol portal was much lower than what he was going. He instinctly realized he had issued at least one bad ticket that day (the first one he had written) but did not understand how or why. Can the reader figure out what happened?

The biggest problem with moving radar is false readings. The next biggest problem is poorly trained or unqualified operators. You may have noted both times Officer Neckvein had a false reading, he was overtaking a truck. Remember beam "B?" It's job was to spread out and bounce off of signs, trees, or anything else that was standing still and then return so that the radar unit could determine the speed of the police car. Beam "B" ran into a little bit of a problem. As it started to spread out, most of it struck the 8 foot by 12 foot metal wall that was the back of the truck that Officer Neckvein was overtaking.

If Officer Neckvein was traveling at 60 mph and the truck was traveling at 35 mph, beam "B" would give a readout of 25 mph for the patrol car.

60 (Neckvein) − 35 (truck) = 25

If the other car was going 75 mph then beam "A" would correctly tell the computer that the closing speed of the two cars was 135 mph.

60 (Neckvein) + 75 (violator) = 135 (closing speed)

The radar unit would then take the incorrect police car speed that was supplied by beam "B" and subtract it from the correct closing speed of the two vehicles, that was supplied by beam "A."

135 − 25 = 105

The radar readout supplied to Officer Neckvein would indicate 105 mph in the portal designated "Violator" and 25 mph in the portal designated as

"Patrol." Had Officer Neckvein known what he was doing, or paid attention in class, he would have known that the reason for the portal marked "Patrol" is so the officer can make sure the unit is giving a proper reading. That readout should always match the speed of the police car.

As if you don't have enough to worry about, there is also a moving radar that points toward the rear and clocks vehicles overtaking the patrol car from behind. I won't go into explaining how this one works but keep in mind that a police car might have this capability. (The units are not all that common.)

If you're in view of a police car, and a truck is close by, stay near it. The large mass of metal will often "hide" your car, or at least cause the radar to take longer to lock in on you. That would give you more time to slow down. Remember too that, unless extraordinary circumstances exist, you need not slow to the speed limit, only to under the cop's tolerance. Also remember, if a cop is "flying low," chances are he won't be able to get a reading on you at all.

Now that you know what dangers you can expect from radar, let's look at a few other speed catching technologies presently in use by police. The first that comes to mind is a little gem known as the speed computer. When purchasing equipment most police agencies turn their noses up at these, in favor of radar units. Count your blessings! In the hands of a competent operator, a speed computer unit can be deadly.

Unlike radar, it does not put out a beam of electromagnetic waves that can activate a detector. It puts out no beam at all. It can be in the process of clocking you while you are not even in view of the cop. It can clock you while you are coming toward the cop, overtaking him from behind, or even while you are in front of him, going in the same direction. As if that is not enough, the officer can pick a spot, well off the highway but where he can see two different stretches of the road and be able to measure the average speed of cars that travel between those two points, in either direction.

Why do we not find speed computers in more common use? I can only tell you that machines using the concept were in operation as long ago as the early seventies. To the cop's regret, the make and model that was quite prominent tended to have an inordinate amount of down time. In fact, many units were broken more often than they were operational. After finding themselves in the position of having to spend big bucks to repair almost new equipment, police budget makers tended to lean toward radar units with a proven track record of less costly repairs. In addition, when a speed computer unit was being repaired, the car was also out of service. When radar units broke, they could be packaged up and shipped to a repair point, but the car stayed operational.

I believe those early prototype units were just ahead of their time. As the name indicates a speed computer needs a computer to operate and with the massive changes in the industry during the last two decades, it is a certainty that units manufactured today are as reliable as any radar unit. Perhaps you have heard of these devices referred to as "Vascar."

That is the registered trademark name for one of the more popular units.

As was pointed out by the antics of Officer Neckvein, a poorly trained radar operator can take a properly working radar unit and create chaos. It is even worse with a speed computer. To get an accurate readout, it is imperative that the operator be not only properly trained but committed to accuracy. Because the unit is totally dependent on the information that the officer supplies, the accuracy of the results are only as good as the officer chooses them to be by his actions. That's enough to scare the hell out of everyone, isn't it?

At any rate, the speed computer works on the basic concept that is the accepted mathematical definition of speed.

Speed = distance × time

The unit can be as simple as two buttons and two toggle switches. Again, in the interest of simplicity, we will refer to the toggle switches as switch "A" and switch "B." We will also refer to the buttons as button "A" and button "B". The sole function of the buttons is to remove some information from the computer that was placed there by one of the toggle switches.

Switch "A" is used to measure distance. It is hooked up to the odometer (speedometer) of the police car. When the toggle is switched on (up) it begins to measure the distance that the police car travels. It continues to measure distance until the toggle is switched off. That distance is then stored in the computer until it is needed. Let us call that distance the length between point "X" and point "Y." The amount of distance does not matter but the longer the distance, the less margin of error exists.

The other toggle switch measures time, just like a stop watch. As your car passes point "X," the officer just switches the "B" toggle on, switching it off when your car reaches point "Y." The computer now has a set distance and the amount of time it took your car to go that distance. Presto! Your average speed for the distance that was in the computer is then displayed on an L. E. D. display for the officer.

To clear the computer for another use, the officer has two options. If he presses button "A," it will cancel both the speed and the distance out of the computer. He must then put a new distance into the computer with his patrol car to use the speed computer again. If he chooses to push button "B," only your time will be removed from the computer but the distance will stay. He then will just use the speed toggle switch (Switch "B") to enter the amount of time it takes for the next potential victim to travel between the same point "X" and "Y," in either direction.

What makes the unit so versatile is the fact you can put the speed and distance into the computer at the same time, rather than in sequence. You can also enter a speed and then put the distance into the computer. If you are still following this, you know the officer will not get a readout until both speed and distance have been placed into the machine.

Let's fabricate a few scenarios that should help you better understand how this deadly machine works. Assume you are speeding on an interstate highway, and you are approaching a police car. As the cop drives under a bridge, he flips toggle "A" up and his car is now measuring distance. As the two of you pass each other, he reverses the toggle switches. The distance, from the bridge to the point where you passed each other, is now locked into the computer and the time it is taking you to go that distance is then being measured. When the officer sees the shadow of the bridge darken your car, he turns off toggle "B." The computer gives him the average speed you traveled between the point where you pass each other and the bridge. You are caught . . . and after you he comes.

In the next scenario, he is traveling at 60 mph and you are overtaking him from behind because you have been doing 75 mph. Of course you slow down but the cop has been waiting for you and knows you are anxious to again accelerate. He goes under the same bridge and flips the distance toggle (Switch "A"). His computer is now measuring the distance he is traveling. He watches you and as you go under the same bridge, he flips on the time toggle switch (Switch "B").

He then floors his patrol car, traveling in excess of 100 mph. You figure he no longer represents a danger to you and again accelerate to 75 mph. As your car continues to speed, the computer in the cop's car is still measuring the distance he is going and the amount of time it is taking you to travel that distance. A few miles up the road he goes over a small hill that will hide him from your view until you are almost upon him. He stops on the shoulder and flips off toggle "A." The distance, from the bridge to that point is now locked in the computer. As you come over the hill and pass the stopped police car, he turns off toggle "B." The time it took you to travel that distance is also in the computer and he has your average speed.

Keep in mind he can make the unit read any speed he wants by traveling at that speed and flipping both toggles up, then down. He can also get inaccurate readings if he attempts to use his depth perception when judging at what point to flip toggle "B" to start measuring speed. Notice I used the shadow of a bridge in the example. He would not get an accurate reading if he tried to judge the exact moment you were adjacent to a sign or tree. Just like radar, the tool is only as good as the person using it.

Let us now get the Federal Government into the act. How do our elected officials con the taxpayers into purchasing airplanes and helicopters that are not needed? Why do we have a deficit? Perhaps it is because hundreds of thousands of dollars (or perhaps we are talking millions, they won't tell me) are being spent by the Federal Government so a few thousand dollars in fines can be made for the states, all in the name of "highway safety." With deals cut like this, is it no wonder so many people view the Federal Government as an ungainly monster that eats our hard earned money and spits it out for useless projects? I can think of no act done by cops, more wantonly wasteful than using an aircraft to catch speeders. God forbid our Governors, Police

Superintendents and County Sheriffs should be deprived of their air forces. This is how this wasteful little scam is run.

The National Highway Traffic Safety Administration, 400 Seventh Street, S. W., Washington, D. C. 20590, allocates massive amounts of funds for use in "Police Traffic Programs." I attempted to find out exactly how much was involved but nobody wanted to tell me. My letters went unanswered and my telephone calls were an exercise in futility. If you care to try your luck, their number is 1-202-366-9550. Expect to get put on hold and bounced from extension to extension. Anyone who believes that our government works under the concept of "freedom of information" has never dealt with a career civil service employee! At any rate, I did learn that each state is allocated a certain amount based on a "complicated formula" including size, population, and total road miles. It was obvious from the people who would talk to me that these funds can be spent on almost anything the states want, if they can link it to "traffic safety." They are called Section 402 funds and would be better spent on improving dying bridges and roads instead of helicopters, airplanes or exotic police sports cars. Contact your congressman or state, "Office of Highway Safety," if you are in agreement. If we could get those funds redirected, it would reduce your chances of getting a ticket and perhaps improve REAL traffic safety by fixing the roads.

Here is the mechanics of how "the bear in the air" operates. A series of white lines or blocks are painted on the shoulder of the road. Expect to find them at equal distances apart, painted on the passing lane and driving lane shoulders, in both directions. Then, down the road about .2 mile will be an identical set. You may find as many as six or eight of these sets, each one spaced the same distance apart.

Then a speed computer like unit, or simple stop watch is used to time cars as they pass between those white marks. The observer in the airplane will have the amount of time it takes you to go a set distance and again will be able to compute your speed. He must then contact an officer on the ground, via radio, to chase you down and write the ticket. It only took a one hundred thousand dollar aircraft, a fully trained pilot, aviation fuel & repairs, a police observer, and the cop on the ground, to issue that ticket. Can you imagine the added cost to the state if you plead not guilty and require all these people to come testify? Want some good news? Airplane speed traps are easy to avoid. The way to do it is covered in Chapter 9.

CHAPTER 8

Before Leaving Home

Although you have already learned a few tricks and techniques to aid you in avoiding a ticket, there are many more the accomplished speeder should know. This next section will deal with what you can do before ever leaving your driveway or carport that will tend to make the officer want to let you go. A subsequent chapter will deal in driving maneuvers designed to help you avoid getting caught while traveling. Like the chapter on what NOT to say, much of the following contents would seem obvious, yet they are points ignored by most drivers.

The object is to give the cop as many reasons as is possible to want to let you off. While doing that, you will also be trying to do away with anything that might encourage him to write the ticket.

First, examine the complete exterior of the vehicle. While doing so, try to enter the cop's mind.

111

Is there anything visible that might irritate, anger or even just displease the officer? It is important you keep in mind his personality might be the opposite of yours. What you construe as funny might offend him and what you visualize as a noble moral stand, might in his opinion, border on sedation.

Let's first cover the most obvious . . . bumper stickers. If a driver collected presidential memorabilia and proudly displayed a perfect "I like Ike" campaign sign on his rear bumper, he would get caught by the only cop in existence who had always had a loathing hatred of President Dwight D. Eisenhower. That is life. Call it Murphy's Law or any other name you choose to give it. We all know that what we least want to happen, usually does. There is not much room for opinions that would be safe. In fact, almost every bumper sticker now in existence might prove offensive to someone. You will have to find something else to hold the rear of the car together.

Political stickers should all be removed. Every politician has voters who are cops that don't like him. The cutesy stickers like: "Don't like my driving, dial 1 800 EAT SHIT" or "Protected by Smith and Wesson" are also best removed and discarded. The "MAFIA Staff car" or "U toucha my car, I breaka your face" stickers will guarantee the police officer who pulls you over will be of Italian descent and have a name like Capone or Luciano. In addition, he will have just come from a family reunion where that very bumper sticker was the source of an angry conversation. What can I tell you, that's life. You can use your car as a forum for your opinions or you can use it to speed. It is not a good idea to try both.

Do you remember in Chapter 4, I mentioned that certain professional groups tended to be given a break. Included in the list were medical and emergency workers such as firemen, ambulance crews, rescue workers, doctors and nurses? You might want to try to cash in on their good fortune by putting on a bumper sticker that would insinuate you were part of one of these groups. I am partial to the ones that say:

MY OTHER CAR IS A FIRE TRUCK
or
MY OTHER CAR IS AN AMBULANCE
or
MY OTHER CAR IS A RESCUE VAN
or
NURSES SAVE LIVES

I know of no law that requires you to be a member of any group before using a bumper sticker. If the cop makes the wrong assumption, shame on him.

While checking the rest of your car, let's not overlook those little yellow diamond shaped signs with the suction cups. At first, all of them just said "Baby on Board" but then the humor started. If you have one that says "Ex-husband in trunk," you can bet the cop will be recently divorced. If you have one that says "Mother-in-law in trunk," he will have just had a fight with his wife, concerning his mother. Get rid of anything that might offend anyone!

The latest hobby has many drivers filling the rear window with baseball type caps. I always felt it was a pretty silly hobby but to each their own. If you are one who takes pride in his hat collection and must display it as mentioned, you should again keep in mind that some of those hats might also be offensive to the cop. If you have a cap advertising any sport team, you can bet the cop will favor their division rival. The use of caps with police logos only indicate to the officer, you were intending in advance, to speed. Those hats also tend to reduce your vision through your rear view mirror and, if you want the best advice, get rid of them.

We can't forget to look at our license plates! It seems there are more cars with vanity plates than cars without them. Does your vanity tag say something that will incur the wrath of the good Knight Sir Paperhanger? Keep in mind, anything that might be insulting, pro-speeding, or linked to any type of substance abuse (including alcohol) should be avoided.

Is the paint faded and does a dent exist in the rear quarter panel? If you intend to spend a lot of time on the open road with the car, I would suggest you have the scratches and dents repaired. Put a good wax job on the car. Always try to get the car washed before any long trip. It is easier to ticket a bum than a "nice guy." Would you go for a job interview in a dirty sweatshirt? You want to make the best impression possible on the cop. Usually the sociopaths who give cops a bad time have filthy, poorly maintained cars. A clean car will be one of those small points that tend to help reduce his fear.

Even if your car is a tired old bomb, you will want to make it look as good as possible. This means you will have to go to a junkyard and replace that missing hubcap that you lost in 1982.

It is also time to fix that leaky muffler system and be certain you replace any tires that look the slightest bit worn. If you were a cop, would you be inclined to give a guy a break who you caught speeding on a bad tire, that might blow at any time, causing an accident?

Do I have to tell you to replace any cracked windows? You want to give the impression you are a responsible individual. How you keep your car tells much about you. The officer may not even realize it, but all these things help contribute to his decision as to who to ticket. If your state requires a vehicle inspection and you are due, or nearly due, get it done before your trip. If you were a cop, would you be inclined to let a car go that you believed had good brakes or one that you suspected might have bad ones?

While you are getting all these repairs done, don't forget to have any rust spots sanded and painted. This may be running into more money than you desire to spend. If you were to consider what a couple of tickets will do to your insurance rate, you might view the repairs as a good investment. In addition, any amount you spend on the car should be recouped when you sell it. You won't get a rebate on any dollars spent in traffic court.

Let's not overlook your car windows. Are there any decals that might be offensive to the cop? The decals that most frequently raise the hackles on cop necks are the ones relating to the musical groups such as "The Grateful Dead." I grant you it's a free country, and you should be free to display any decal you want but the police who patrol most of the interstates have, every summer, run into a group of people who are known collectively as "The Deadheads." Many of those people travel from city to city following the Grateful Dead's concert tours.

When they come through, it's as if we were transported back to the 1960's. Tie-dyed clothing and Volkswagen vans with peace signs are seen in abundance. I always enjoyed watching them pass through. The average "deadhead" is so laid back, you could describe them as docile. Most cops dislike them because of the drugs that seem to be part of their lifestyle yet I have never seen a "deadhead" give a cop any trouble. They just want to be left alone to "do their thing." Because of the potential for drugs, most cops abhor their presence.

Do you have any decals that indicate you support a particular Police Benevolent Association or other cop fraternal outfit? Let me now uncover one of the biggest rip offs the public has ever seen. I refer to "honorary" membership in these organizations. Is this ever going to make me some enemies in the police ranks!!

Police Benevolent Associations exist for almost every police agency. Some are just what they appear to be; a fraternal organization dedicated to its members well-being. In most of the other cases, they are unions, organized labor, nothing more and nothing less. They charge dues and supply union type benefits for their members. They often are the sole negotiators of police contracts and they represent their members in contract grievances.

To increase their positive cash flow, they sell "honorary" membership in their organizations. For your donation you will usually receive a decal to put on your car window and a membership card for your wallet or purse. The card will ask "any officer to extend to the holder every courtesy. . . ." It is also a good bet that you will end up on the mailing lists of other similar cop organizations. A year later you can be certain that the P. B. A. will send you a reminder that your card has expired and they will require payment for the renewal of your "honorary" membership. The only thing being honored is the almighty dollar. As for the cop "extending every courtesy," that is exactly what a large portion of a cop's job is! He is paid to help people.

Naturally, you will be under the mistaken impression the decal and card will help you get out of a ticket. Notice the exact words I used were "mistaken impression." Let's be honest. Everyone knows what you are trying to purchase. Would you give a yearly donation to the Teamster's Union if they promised you a decal and courtesy card? If the cops just sent you a thank you letter but no decal or card, would you be so anxious to part with your money?

It boils down to this; will the police officer who stops you, let you go because you gave money to a police union? Keep in mind that his union is probably not even the same one that got your donation. Would a union carpenter reduce his bill for you if he knew you had donated money to a steamfitter's union?

Sure, it is possible that the card in your hand will keep the speeding ticket from being written. It is just as likely it will guarantee you'll get a ticket! Let me explain. Police unions, like all other unions, have members who are happy with the union's actions and members who are not. If you were pulled over by a P.B.A. delegate (the officer representative, like a shop steward) then, chances are he might be inclined to let you go. If you were pulled over by someone who was not happy with the last contract, or recently lost a contract dispute, the "honorary" card might have the opposite effect. For the majority of cops, the attitude they have when you present them with the card is: "Does this SOB think he can buy his way out of this ticket?!" This attitude is reinforced every time someone gets pulled over and starts waving a handful of courtesy cards representing different P.B.A.s, in the cop's face.

Cop unions and P.B.A.s do a lot of good work and have been of tremendous assistance when officers have faced false accusations and law suits. If you feel it is the right thing to do, by all means help these organizations. I just don't recommend you display the card when you are stopped. As far as the decal on the window is concerned, it could help and it could hurt. You will have to make your own decision but it never helped anyone I pulled over.

There is an exception to every rule. A "P.B.A." card will often work if when handed to the cop, the driver mentions he was given the card by a good friend, Officer————. This gives the cop a different outlook on the whole matter. You are no longer trying to bribe your way out of a ticket. You have become the friend of some fellow officer who is saying, ''This is my friend. Don't paper him.''

Shall we now enter the inside of your vehicle? Just as when we were discussing the exterior of your car, neatness counts. For starters, clean the floors and under the seats. Get rid of any old beer, soda bottles or trash. The presence of an empty beer bottle telegraphs to the cop, ''This guy sometimes drinks while he is driving.'' Is that the message you want to give to the cop as he is asking for your license and registration?

Consider removing all those items hanging from your rear view mirror. It might be something as minor as your wife's wedding garter but most of the time they are feathers attached to clips called roach holders. Do you want a cop to suspect you smoke marijuana? Leave these foolish decorations hanging and that is exactly what he will think. It won't matter that your sweetheart gave it to you after winning it at a carnival. The cop will make his assumptions and never consider asking you about their validity.

Empty the ash tray and get into the habit of closing it when not in use. If you smoke, vacuum it out whenever you wash the car. The cop will make it a point to look at the ash tray. He will be looking for marijuana roaches or a pipe. If it is left open and is full, the cop will count about two points in the ''slob'' column while attempting to decide what kind of person you are. This may seem like we are covering some very minor things yet the sum total of all these minor things is what affects the cop's final decision.

Then there's your glove box. You will remember I recommended you leave it opened if you were stopped? You will want to give the impression of a "neat" person. Clean out the glove box of all unnecessary items. When you leave it open, the cop should be able to look into it and be certain there is no contraband. If there is a gun in a car, the two most likely places will be in the glove box or under the driver's seat. By having a clean, nearly empty glove box, and casually displaying it to the cop, you have reduced his fear by a large percentage. Don't forget to take out any contraband that you do have or this little ploy will backfire. Do not store any small closed containers or items wrapped in tin foil. I don't know why but it is amazing how often bullets and fireworks are left in there. Get rid of anything that will arouse his curiosity or interest. You want to be a bit boring.

If you have any packages in the car it would be a good idea to see if you can leave the tops open. This will enable him to look inside and will also satisfy his curiosity or concerns. If you are transporting beer or liquor, do it in the trunk.

If you must transport weapons in the car, either put them in a closed container or be certain that no bullets are visible. Have the action of any weapons open in such a manner that the cop can be sure the gun is not loaded. If at all possible, carry the weapons in the trunk. Never have them within reach as you sit in the driver's seat. Owners of pickup trucks, keep those gun racks empty if you plan to speed.

Are you all paying attention? The single, most important reason why some speeders get tickets while others are let go, is soon to be revealed. I will also soon tell you how to put yourself on the side of the ones that get away. Be patient. It will take me a few paragraphs to explain.

When I decided this book would be written, I knew it would be in the reader's best interest if I could interview other officers. I felt, then as now, that the opinions I had were valid yet they were just that . . . only my opinions. It was no easy effort to interview other officers without letting them know what I was really doing or why. Needless to say, to have let my bosses find out what I intended to do would have made life rather uncomfortable for me before I retired. Although most of these clandestine interviews only verified what I already knew, one point was so strongly voiced in every conversation, even I was quite surprised.

Every officer was adamant that anyone stopped for speeding, who was equipped with a radar detector, would get a ticket. Many of the officers even go so far as to denote on the ticket which drivers were equipped, in the belief that the judge would be less inclined toward granting a reduction. Before you run out to the car and rip out your unit, read on!

Just why are the cops so vehement when it comes to radar detectors? It can't be because they work great or people with detectors would not be getting caught. There are two reasons why the feathers get ruffled on the cop when the radar detector is seen.

To begin with, you are instantly labeled as a blatant speeder. Your speeding is premeditated or you wouldn't have the thing in your car in the first place. Speeding is just so important to you that you are prepared to shell out a couple of hundred bucks to decrease your chances of getting caught.

I know all the hype presented in the advertisements about how you must protect yourself from faulty radar units and poorly trained operators. You and I both know what hype this is! If you are going to get an undeserved ticket for speeding, how is the possession of a radar detector going to help you, except to warn you that radar is ahead? What do you then do? You slow down! If the radar unit was faulty or the operator poorly trained, you would get a ticket anyway! The possession of the radar detector is then of no use, for that reason.

If you pulled speeders over for a living, it would not take you long to notice that the vast majority of the speeding cars were equipped with radar detectors, and those going at or below the speed limit did not have the device. It is simple for the cop to know who you are. It's time for a "war story" to make a point.

When radar detectors first began to enter the market, I was working on Interstate 81, near Syracuse, N.Y. I was also fortunate to have assigned to me an unmarked car, paid for by the Federal Government, designed to look as little like a police car as was possible. All the troop cars at the time were Dodges and this was a Chrysler Newport with a beige vinyl top, white walls, sporty wheel covers, a "regular" license plate and a few other tricks. It was a traffic ticket writer's dream come true.

I was cruising along in the driving lane when a car passed me at a speed of about 75 mph. On this dashboard, in plain view was a radar detector. I pulled directly behind the car and we both cruised along for a mile or so. I could have stopped him and just given him a ticket after clocking him but what fun would that have been? I turned on the radar gun that was laying on the seat next to me. The inside of the violators car began to flash on and off as he stabbed his brakes while pulling to the right lane. I did the same and turned off the radar unit.

The unit was no sooner turned off when the dummy began to accelerate again. In no time we were back in the passing lane at 75 mph. You guessed it! I just couldn't help myself. I again turned on the radar unit, his car again lit up as the radar detector activated and again we both pulled to the right lane, while slowing to the speed limit. I was, by now, laughing so hard it was difficult to keep the car on the road. Watching the man was no help in regaining my self-control as he craned his neck left and right, looking for the cop car. Who could resist? I turned off the radar until we were soon back in the passing lane at 75 mph.

Just as the man was starting to relax, it was "déjà vu" time as I again activated the radar. Back to the right lane we went, as our cars again slowed down to 55 mph. I must admit it, by now I had lost all self-control and tears of laughter were rolling down my face. It was about time to totally ruin this guy's day.

Just so there would be no doubt in this fool's mind that he had been caught with his pants down, I turned off the radar unit, knowing we would again soon be zipping along at 75 mph. It didn't take long at all. When we were once more in the passing lane at 75, I activated my flashing grill lights, headlights and siren, instantly regretting doing so as I realized I would always wonder how many times I could have made him slow down and speed up.

Once he was pulled over and I had his license in my hand, my personality would not permit me to just write the ticket without rubbing salt in his wounds. I told him how long I had been behind him and with the dumbest look I could muster, told him there must be something wrong with his newfangled electronic brakes. When he asked me what I was talking about, I innocently told him I didn't know what the warning light on his dash meant but every time I turned on my radar, I could see he was having trouble because his brakes would lock up and pull him to the right. He was also told he was lucky I was smart enough to keep turning off the radar or he might have had an accident. The last thing I said before turning back to my car was, "Whatever it is, you better get that contraption fixed because police radar seems to affect it."

Two steps later the noises behind me caused me to regret my foolishness. The sounds made me positive this guy was getting out of his car with the intent to do me no small amount of bodily harm. I whirled around, crouching into a defensive posture with my hand gripping the handle of my revolver, only to see the man was making no effort to come after me. He was just sitting there, oblivious to me. The noise was from him repeatedly banging his head against the steering wheel.

What points am I trying to bring out? First, you can bet the only reason this guy bought his radar detector was to speed and that's why most everyone buys one. It would be foolish to expect the cop to think differently. Second, cops can see radar detectors in your car and when the lights are illuminated, they may also be visible to the cop, especially at night. Third, the cop can often make the determination that you have a radar detector because of the manner in which you drive.

You must figure out a way to keep your radar detector while making it invisible to the cop. I mentioned there were two reasons why cops hate the radar detector so much. The first reason was that it indicated the driver had premeditation. The second reason is, if someone knows how to properly use one, it can be a big help in avoiding getting caught. It is too valuable a tool for you to relinquish. If you have one, keep it. If you do not have one, go out and buy the best one you can afford.

The first thing to do is get out some black paint or tape and cover the small lights on the back of the unit. They are often visible to every cop coming up behind you. If his radar unit is off and he sees you going a little over the limit, the sight of those lights might get you stopped and ticketed. I am also referring to the light indicating the unit is on, usually a small green one. Were he not to see those lights or the telltale cord, he might not bother to even stop you. Remember, if you are stopped, it is almost always from behind and you will not have time to hide the unit. People who try always arouse the cop's suspicion that something else is being hidden. Cops have an excellent view of your car's interior when pulling you over from behind. You should be turning on your inside light and sitting still, remember?

You must also hide the twisty cord that hangs down in plain view from your detector. It is a simple matter to run the cord under the interior body molding that runs between the side of the windshield and the driver's door. Most of the time, it only requires the loosening of a couple of screws. Now you can only hope the cop will not bend his head over and look up for the receiver. The closer you mount the receiver to the driver's side of the car, the more difficult it is for the cop to notice it. Your best bet is to have one installed that has the antenna mounted in the grill and the receiver mounted inside the car but out of sight.

Remember, I told you the officer will always look at your ash tray, to check for marijuana? Where is your radar detector plugged in? His radar unit works the same way. If you are going to the expense of purchasing a radar detector, you should also be willing to go to the small expense of having it installed with its own power source, other than the cigarette lighter. It is cheap and easy to have another electrical connection installed, under the dashboard, out of sight. Do it right or expect the unit to be more of a liability than an asset. Whatever action you can take to keep the officer from seeing you are equipped with a radar detector will help you. I should also point out that if you think you can gain absolution by turning it off and telling the cop you were not using it, forget it. Like the marijuana pipe or empty beer bottle; to the cop, if you possess the item, you do the dirty deed. If you have the detector in the car and he sees it, the cop will consider you an intentional speeder.

One more action you can take to help yourself is when purchasing a car, avoid the trendy accessory of heavily tinted side windows. If your car already has those windows, it would be well worth the cost and effort to have them replaced with the standard type. Cops hate them. You have limited the officer's ability to look into the car thus reducing his chances of avoiding any possible danger that might be lurking in your back seat. He will be nervous and resentful before you even have a chance to greet him. Rather than reducing his fear, you will have been elevating it.

Most of the cars that have these windows are models that also have electric power windows so you do have another alternative. Before the cop exits his car, roll ALL of your car's windows down, even if you are alone. This lights up the inside of your car and reduces his anxiety.

CHAPTER 9

Travel—From Blast Off
To Landing

So you are now ready to put the car in gear and begin your trip. Wrong again! You will first have to decide when is the best time to leave. Are you wondering, "What difference could that possibly make?" It could mean the difference between your getting a ticket or possibly avoiding one, which this book is supposed to show you. Would it not be foolish if you did not take advantage of every possibility for reducing the mathematical probability of a ticket being written? We can begin with the date. No, I am not into numerology but you better believe the date is very important. The best day to travel is the fifteenth of any month and the worst days would be the first or last few days of the month. As you approach the fifteenth, your chances of getting a ticket are reduced and after the fifteenth, they increase more and more each day. Do you think this is ridiculous? What difference could the date make? I guess an explanation is again in order.

Cops are like everyone else. Some are lazy and tend to procrastinate. Others are just the opposite. You have heard cops have a quota system and that is, in some respects, quite true. If you think about it, every job is based on some type of quota system. If you work an assembly line making widgets and you make less widgets than anyone else, you can expect to get fired. The C.E.O. of a company that makes much less profit than the stockholders anticipated, can also expect to soon pull the cord on his golden parachute.

The productivity of police is usually checked monthly and is compared to the same month in the previous year. They may not be expected to write a specific number of tickets each day but they better have the proper "monthly average." Those who are often below average manage to incur the wrath of their supervisors. Those who write the most tickets generally are given some type of preferential treatment.

Because of this policy, the procrastinating cops often find themselves in a position that requires they "catch up" their ticket writing at the end of the month. Their more aggressive brothers have written their tickets at the beginning of the month. During the first week of the month, the aggressive cops often reach the maximum number of tickets they dare write. If these cops write too many tickets, they will incur the wrath of the less dedicated brethren. As a result, the safest day to travel is the fifteenth of the month.

Now that you know what day to travel, could it possibly matter what time to travel? Certainly! You should plan to reach the interstate highway at about thirty minutes prior to the end of the cop's tour of duty. This does present a bit of a problem. It wouldn't do to call up the Highway Patrol or Sheriff's Office and say, "I'm planning to take a trip and would like to get a good fast start. Could you tell me when you folks change shifts?"

If you pick up a newspaper and look for an officer's name, you will find they are included with most reports of accidents. It would be easy to call up and ask for that cop by name. If he is working, chances are he will be out on the road and they will tell you when to call back. If he is working the next shift, they will tell you when he is coming to work. Presto. You now know the time of shift change. If you are unlucky and he is there, just tell him you are a citizen and want to express your appreciation after reading in the paper about his great job at the accident. After you hang up, find another cop's name in the paper and try again.

It would also be best if you avoided the morning when planning to travel and began at the end of the cop's day shift or in the late afternoon. As mentioned before, there is very little that police supervisors can use as rewards or positive reinforcement for the cops that work hard. One thing supervisors can do is assign the hard workers to a preferred shift. As a result, most special details are assigned during the day shift. The importance to you is obvious. More cops working means more chances for you to get caught. In addition, there is a likely possibility that the cops assigned to the day shift are the ones who tend to write the most tickets. If you can avoid the day shift by traveling later in the day, then by all means, do so.

There is a sacred tradition among police. Any tour of duty cannot begin without being certain that the coffee shop is safe from any danger. The only way the police can be sure their coffee shop is safe is to congregate there. As long as they are all together, they might as well have a cup of coffee, a donut and shoot the breeze for a while. For the first half hour to forty-five minutes of each shift, the most likely spot of concentrated police presence is not on the interstate highway. During the last half hour of the previous shift, most cops are at their station, filling out paperwork. Does it take a genius to realize that this is when it is safest to speed?

Knowing the officers will procrastinate before beginning their patrol and knowing when the shift change takes place will enable you to pull off another coup. Like other devious tricks, it takes some devious planning. Find out where the police stations, sheriffs' offices, or trooper barracks are that serve the road you plan to travel. The coffee shops should be located in close proximity to the station. After the necessary coffee and pastry, the officer will be patrolling directly away from his station, to the end of his post. If he has a subsequent post, he also will have to travel in the same direction (away from the station) to reach it.

If you can arrange your trip so you pass the exit

where the police station is located, at about shift change then the cops beginning work will be behind you, going the same direction you are going. Now that's not a bad place to leave them, if you get my drift. They will also be obligated to stop to assist any disabled vehicles you drive past so, chances are they will never catch up to you. Any stragglers you meet from the previous shift, coming toward you, will tend to ignore you because they want to go home.

If you ever find yourself approaching an exit during the hour after shift change, BEWARE!!! The cops who are beginning their shift will be coming at you, making you a perfect target for moving radar.

While we are on the subject of where and when to expect cops, have you ever slowed down, and continued to go slow after passing two police cars parked next to each other, facing in opposite directions in the median? You almost had a free pass to speed and didn't use it! Police work can get very boring and lonesome. Does that seem illogical? The public views police work as exciting and fast paced. I have heard it better described as long periods of boredom, interrupted by short bursts of terror! One of the reasons officers can be expected to congregate at coffee shops is because they know it is unlikely they will have much of a chance to socialize with their cohorts during the remainder of their tour. Most of the time they have no one to talk to except violators. Unlike the CB, their radio does not permit chatting.

So, if you find two of their cars parked in the

median, the odds are you are at the edge of two posts or areas of patrol. The odds also are the cops responsible for those posts are going to continue to sit in the median "chewing the fat" for quite a while. For the next ten to fifteen miles it will be unlikely you will have any police type company. When the cop who is responsible for the post area you will be entering pulls out, he will be behind you. Just watch your rear view mirror for any car overtaking yours at a high rate of speed and enjoy your free pass.

To a degree the same holds true whenever you pass a solitary patrol in the opposite direction but a word of caution is advised. You will have no way of knowing if you are about to enter another post or if the car you passed was the post car. He may have been a transient, such as a prisoner transport.

Every once in a while, some high ranking police brass get it into their collective, freeze-dried brains that they can get free publicity by saturating a piece of road with cops. Even they realize there are insufficient resources to maintain the same high level of coverage for more than a short time. Yet, like a cat sensing an injured bird, they smell the heady aroma of press coverage. Is it possible that, after years of strutting with their noses in the air, concerned more with their next promotion than police work, that these people actually convince themselves you will slow down the next time you travel that road? They even coined a name for this particular wanton waste of taxpayer's dollars. It is called speed saturation and the subsequent statistics always look great because the cops reduce their tolerance.

It has even become multi-agency with neat military names like "Operation Co-Flame." Whenever adults act like children, they should be ashamed of themselves, especially if they waste hard earned tax dollars in the process.

So what's your defense for this collective act of taxpayer waste and stupidity? An inexpensive CB radio will again, work fine. If you hear multiple reports of speed traps or police activity in any given area, slow down to the speed limit for at least one half hour of travel. It's important to remember that these assinine special details are one of the few times the police reduce the "tolerance." What would you do if your boss was breathing down your neck demanding results? Remember, if the reported police activity in any given area seems unusually high, you should suspect a "speed saturation" and slow down until out of that area. Because of the prohibitive expense, these farces are only held often enough to get the attention of the press.

Let's now consider traveling in the dead of night. There are some distinct advantages and disadvantages. The disadvantages are obvious. With less people on the road to warn you of police presence with their CB radios and with the cover of darkness favoring them, police can get pretty sneaky. The advantages are twofold. There are fewer cops working the "graveyard" shift than at any other time and some of the cops that are working spend at least part of the shift sleeping.

To give you an idea of the difference that exists, let us look at the post assignments on a 152 mile segment of the New York State Thruway (I-90), beginning at milepost 198, located between the cities of Albany and Utica, and stretching to the edge of Rochester at milepost 350. This road is considered one of the best policed roads in the U.S.A. and is patrolled exclusively by the New York State Police. On an average, there are 10 patrols working during the day, 7 patrols in the evening and only 4 patrols between midnight and 5 A.M.

If you are lucky, one of the patrols will be sleeping and one will be tied up with an arrest. That would mean you could expect to see one patrol every 75 miles. If one of those two remaining cars has someone pulled over when you drive by, then you will have one chance in 150 miles of getting caught. The car containing Officer Sleeping Beauty might even be so kind as to keep his radar unit turned on so your detector will tell you his approximate whereabouts.

Still other advantages exist in traveling during the middle of the night. The cops that are working are not expected to write as many tickets as those working other shifts. They tend to permit higher tolerances and often only choose to chase the most flagrant violators.

As long as we are talking about night driving, now might be a good time to cover spotlighting. No, I am not referring to that slightly less than sporting method of harvesting deer at night. Spotlighting is the unofficial practice by the interstate cop of shining his spotlight across the median and onto an approaching violator so as to be able to later identify the car when he catches up with it. It is used in conjunction with moving radar. It is not the sort of thing that you might expect to be covered in a police academy curriculum because of the danger of civil liability. It can be very dangerous if not done properly but is quite simple to do and does not take very long to master. To avoid blinding the violator, the cop must turn on the spotlight at or after the point where the two cars are opposite each other.

If done too soon, the violator (who, don't forget, is speeding) will be blinded. If done properly, the violator only experiences a flicker of intense light out of the corner of his eye. Most times he does not even realize what caused it. Because of the combined speed of the two cars and because the light is not directed into the violator's eyes, it is over so fast that the light is gone before the driver can react. Don't mistake a police car sitting in a U-turn area with his lights so directed as to illuminate the cars going by. This is also done but it is more likely they are looking for drug runners in a practice known as profiling. If a person fits the drug runner profile or appears suspicious for other reasons, the cops will pull out and follow him.

Now that spotlighting has been described to you, should it happen, you will probably know what it is instantly. So how should you react if you are spotlighted? You have a number of options. Keep in mind a cop would not be inclined to spotlight you unless his intent was to stop you. This is not a comforting thought is it? There's an outside chance he may be looking for some other specific vehicle reportedly heading toward him but that is not likely. No matter what your decision, making it in advance, prior to being spotlighted is in your best interest. The way I see it, you have about four options.

Option #1: Try to outrun the cop car. This book has been based on how to outsmart the police officer. If you are stupid enough to take the chance at trying to outrun a cop, then it is obvious this book is beyond your mental capability so please give it to someone else who can appreciate it. I'm not saying that, under the proper conditions it can't be done. I am saying it is a bad decision based on the danger involved.

Option #2: Unconditional surrender. Don't dismiss this one out of hand. Japan surrendered to us and look where they are today. By surrendering, you have created the best chance of talking your way out of the ticket. You will be in the very best position of reducing the cop's fear and building his ego. What could possibly build a guy's ego more than having his opponent concede defeat? The cop will again suspect you are another police officer until he has interviewed you. If this seems like a viable alternative to you, just pick a safe spot, on a straight and level part of the road and pull over before the officer even catches up to you. Pull well onto the shoulder, putting into practice everything you were taught about the positioning of your car. Leave your headlights on, turn on your inside light and activate your emergency flashers.

If the cop does not show up behind you in about two or three minutes, resume your trip. Chances are he could not find a convenient U-turn and changed his mind about chasing you. This can happen quite often, depending on the composition of the median in that area.

Option #3: This one is for those of you who want to try being crafty. Watch the cop's car in the rear view mirror. It must disappear from view before starting to U-turn for this trick to have a chance at working. As soon as his car is out of sight, slow down as fast as you can without leaving skid marks. Pull as far as you can off the right side of the road and turn off all your lights, both interior and exterior. Put the seat as far back as it will go and the head rest up. Now close your eyes and do your best to look as if you have been sleeping for a while. Nice little touches like a blanket pulled up around you and your teddy bear will go a long way here. Be certain that you remember to turn off the car's engine or you won't fool anyone.

The cop car will come up on your darkened vehicle with its afterburners just a-glowing. When the driver sees you, he must initiate one of two courses of action and must decide instantly. He can decide you are not the intended victim and continue to rocket down the highway or he will lock up his brakes, pull the cord on his drag chute, and do his best at trying to stop before passing you. If he chooses to stop, be sure you sleep through the screaming brakes and the cloud of smoke caused by his locked up tires.

You will continue to sleep until he taps on your driver's side window. At this point you can thank your lucky stars if you took acting lessons. You also must follow these instructions exactly. You will be startled but not too startled. You will jerk your head, just a little bit while opening your eyes. Stare straight ahead, out the windshield, with a blank look, sort of like a poor zombie imitation. This should last about two to three seconds. You then slowly turn your head to the left and are again startled as you see the cop. Slowly roll down your window and say, "I fell asleep, what time is it?" as you lift your hand to try to look at your watch in the darkness.

If he asks how long you have been there, say you are unsure, maybe about fifteen minutes or a half hour. Don't be specific or claim more time because he may have recently patroled right past this spot. He would also only need to place his hand on your warm car hood to blow a big hole in your story if you claimed to have been there half the night. Keep in mind, this is just a trial. You don't have to prove your innocence, only create a reasonable doubt. If the cop is not sure, he will give you that benefit of that doubt and you just won!

Just like in option #2, if the cop fails to show up within about three minutes, continue your trip and count your blessings as you just had a close call. There is one more point to consider. If the cop fails to show, he may have radioed another car about you. That next car might make a special effort to catch you so slow down for a while.

Before we move on to option #4, in the interest of covering all bases, there is one more point to consider. What do you do if the police car does blast by you without stopping? You take a fifteen minute nap, that's what you do! If you resume your trip right away, you may find the cop waiting for you just up the road. If he catches you trying to sneak away, flames and smoke may be seen coming from his nostrils. Play it safe and have a nice nap. Won't it be worth the wasted time, knowing you got the best of Smokey?

Shall we now reveal your fourth option? It's used so often that it does not work very well. I'm referring to the, "It wasn't me officer, it was the other guy" ploy. Simply continue to drive but stay at the speed limit until the cop pulls you over. When he tells you that you were speeding say, "That wasn't me, it was the guy behind me that you lit up with your spotlight. I saw it all in my rear view mirror. Right after that he went by me like a bat out of hell." Even if you were the only car on the road, if you are adamant enough, and if the cop got less than a perfect look at you, the unwritten rules of the game will require he lets you go, should he have the slightest doubt.

Most of the interstate miles driven by the infrequent traveler is due to vacation or family visits on long holiday weekends. Have you wondered if there is a "best" or "worst" time for weekend travel? Try to structure your travel to be different from what everyone else is doing. By that I mean if most people are traveling on a Thursday evening, you should attempt to get an extra day off work and leave on Wednesday evening. If the majority of return holiday travel is expected on Sunday, then you might plan to return on Saturday or early Monday morning.

The best day of the week for ticket free travel is usually Saturday. Travel is then lightest, and because of this, cops don't often plan to do much traffic work. In addition, the day shift prima donna officers with the special assignments are often given at least part of the weekend off. Other cops who are scheduled for days off just before or just after Saturday, will often request the day off as bonus vacation, personal or sick leave so as to spend more time with their families. The same is true for the Sunday day shift. Fewer cops means fewer tickets issued.

What day of the year is the best to speed? Of course, it is Christmas day. The fewest possible cops are working and those that are, have no desire to do police work.

Before we move on to the next subject, I should mention those press releases given out by Police Superintendents and Commissioners, claiming traffic enforcement is being "stepped up" for the holiday weekend. They are lies, plain and simple. Did you ever notice that the press releases never give specifics about how many more officers or patrols will be out? They use terms like "in force" and "making a concentrated effort," yet avoid exact numbers.

Is it not logical to expect that during a holiday weekend, the maximum number of officers that their contract permits, will be on vacation? Won't all the prima donnas who work days with weekends off, also have the holiday off? You can bet they will! Do you think the use, or abuse of sick leave will decline because the boss puts out a press release?

Even if the big boss is prepared to bring cops in on overtime, if their contract permits it, many cops would decline. If their contract does not permit them to refuse overtime, they will do everything in their power to get the time off. One way or another, many will avoid working. The officers get to spend too little quality time with their families as it is! In addition, consider this: If the cops are ordered in against their will, do you expect them to get right out and patrol aggressively? Cops are not out "in force" on holiday weekends because there are no cops to send out. The patrolling nature of the job makes it nearly impossible for a supervisor to strictly watch the cops. Given that set of circumstances, how hard would you work?

At last, you have the information necessary for you to make an intelligent decision as to when to leave. Your car is designed for ticket avoidance and you are about to mash your foot to the floor in a speeding frenzy. Too bad! You're not ready yet! We still have a few more things to cover. (I just love doing this to you.)

Look down at your lap. Do you expect me to let you start a trip when you are not wearing your seat belt? Get serious! As I have already pointed out; if you are reading this book then you are planning to speed. If you are going to speed and don't have your seat belt on, then something is wrong with your gray matter. There I go again, insulting you. Old habits are just so hard to break. At any rate, let's consider the use of seat belts.

Sure, you have heard all the standard reasons for wearing seat belts, a thousand times. In addition, you are reading this book so as to learn how to avoid getting speeding tickets. What right do I have to start a seat belt sermon? If I manage to draw a correlation, will you at least try to get used to wearing it? You have heard all the standard reasons but here are a couple of reasons I bet most of you never considered. For starters, and the reason I feel the need to bring the subject up in this book, if you are stopped and everyone in the car is belted in, the cop will have a better opinion of you. This will be another reason for you to be considered one of the good guys, a safe driver who just happened to be going a little fast. A driver who deserves to be given a break.

For a unique reason to buckle up consider that it will make you a better driver. While executing any extreme maneuver at high speed, such as is sometimes necessary to avoid an accident, a person not buckled in will be doing more holding than steering with the steering wheel. I am convinced that putting on that seat belt is the best tactic any driver can adopt to improve his ability to avoid accidents. Enough said?

So, at last you are on the paved ribbon with your speedometer needle leaning to the right. The speed of your car, as you roar down the passing lane makes you feel like you are in a new car commercial. Your headlights are on high beam to clear the lane in front of you. A half dozen Madison Avenue generated phrases about the "great feeling" keep running through your head as the sun shines through your sunroof. This just feels so good you can't help but relax a little more, smile and enjoy the ride.

I just don't know how you ever existed before I came along to tell you how many mistakes you keep making. Of course you're at it again. Oh this makes me feel so smug! Please permit me to point out you are making three very big mistakes. You are in the passing lane, your headlights are on and you are relaxing. Any one of the three increase your chances for a ticket.

Never speed with your headlights on during the day. Yes, it does move some of the slower people who don't have smarts enough to stay out of your way. It also instantly brings you to the attention of the cop sitting in the median running radar, or approaching you with moving radar. Because of the advent of the hold button, not every car is clocked. If you have your headlights on in broad daylight, this will almost guarantee that you become one of the chosen few. This is especially important if you are at or near the tolerance limit. If the cop chooses to clock someone else on radar, you will escape unscathed. If he chooses you because your headlights are on, chances are you will get the ticket. You will also be considered one of those intentional speeders and I already told you how cops hate premeditated speeding.

There is a better way to move aside the idiots who clog up the interstate's passing lane, however, driving a snowplow with the wing blade down at 80 mph is not for everyone. As an alternative, turn on your headlights and make sure the high beam switch is activated. Then turn them off. As you approach one of the "turtle type" drivers (I call them turtles because they are always traveling slow and have their head up their . . . er . . . shell), simply flash your headlights at them a couple of times. Because you did not change back to the low beam, your car's high beams will be flashing.

Do this when you are about three to four truck lengths behind them. Yes, I do mean that far. Many of these jerks do not mind getting out of your way but they fail to ever notice you until you have, out of necessity, become one of "those tailgating fools." This type of driver almost always believes it is his sacred duty to "punish" tailgates by not getting out of the way. If they would have moved, had your headlights been on all the time, they will also move if you flash them a few times, from a distance.

Now that your headlights are off, we can cover the basics of lane usage. Quite simply, whenever possible, stay in the lane that is as far to the extreme right as driving conditions permit. If the amount of traffic will make it appear you are weaving in and out, then you will have to temper this requirement but when possible keep to the right. That smacks of driving heresy doesn't it? As far back as your first day in driver education class, the instructor stressed, slower moving traffic stays to the right. It is time for another bomb shell. If you stay to the right, your speed will be reduced by a few miles at most radar traps and especially on moving radar. I bet you can't wait to hear the explanation for this one can you?

Before we go any further, it's important you understand that just one or two miles per hour can make all the difference in the world. If the officer has made the decision that his tolerance will be 70 mph for those traveling in a 55 mph zone, chances are he will use the same tolerance every day. He might write a ticket to someone going 65 mph during very bad weather or when it presents a special hazard, but generally he will always draw the line at 70 mph, the same point. If you are going far in excess of the 70 mph limit and he sees you, yet before he activates his radar you have managed to get below his self-imposed limit, it is very unlikely he will ticket you.

Perhaps I should restate this differently to be certain it is understood. Assume you are traveling at 80 mph. The speed limit is 55 mph and the police in that area have elected to set a tolerance at 70 mph. Your Citizens Band Radio has warned you a cop is coming toward you and your radar detector activated for just a split second a couple of times, as he clocked others with his instant on/off button. You are concentrating on the upcoming traffic, looking for the cop. You know you should have slowed down already yet you are late for a very important meeting and choose to push your luck. Here he comes. You see Officer Neckvein as he crests a hill. You first thought is "Yoicks!" which means "I may have just pushed my luck a little bit too far." "Yoicks" should not be confused with "Oh Shit!" which was explained in an earlier chapter.

Having no other recourse, you spike your brakes. You are slowing but are nowhere near 55 mph when your radar detector activates, telling you Officer Neckvein has your number. If you managed to slow to 69 mph and Neckvein's tolerance is 70 mph, you are free, even though the cop knows you were going in excess of that prior to his hitting you with radar and even though you never reached the "legal" limit of 55 mph. Some officers have even created two different tolerances, one for cars that appear to have radar detectors and another, slightly faster one for cars that do not act as if they are equipped. Unless the cop does not permit any tolerance at all, and if that is so, his trial case load would be gigantic, you do not need to slow as much as you thought. If you stem your brakes so hard that sparks come from your front bumper while trying to reach that magic 55 mph, the cop will know you have a radar detector that just went off. Always try to avoid having to slow down by spiking your brakes in such a way that the deceleration is so obvious.

Try this instead. Take your foot off the gas pedal while pulling your shifter to a lower gear. In most cars that are automatic, there is a second gear or one marked "L-2" that works well. A word of caution should be made here. If you are really flying, it would be better for your car if you just took your foot off the gas pedal but refrained from putting the car in the lower gear. It depends on your car and what transmission you have. If you are in doubt, ask your car mechanic. A good rule of thumb is to consider the lower gear like your passing gear. If you floored the accelerator, would the car go into passing gear at that speed? If the answer is yes, then it should be safe to put the car in the lower gear to slow down. Don't forget to disengage any cruise control.

This will also keep your brake lights from announcing what you are doing if the cop is behind you. Let us say he is clocking you at 71 mph and his tolerance is 70 mph. To be doubly certain of your speed, he turns on his radar unit. Your brakes immediately light up as you slow to 55 mph. You are using a radar detector and he knows it. On the other hand. If you slow to about 62 or 63 mph and your brake lights never go on, he will assume you just realized how-fast you were going and made a correction. If you were in the driving lane, rather than the passing lane when this happened, there is even less chance he will stop you.

While keeping in mind that only one mile per hour may mean the difference between getting a ticket or avoiding one, let us again look at the operation and limitations of a radar unit. You remember that the police radar sends out a series of waves. It then measures the difference in the amount of time it takes each wave to return from the item it bounced off.

Picture a T intersection. You are traveling across the top of the T, it doesn't matter what speed you are going. The officer is sitting at the bottom of the "T" stem with his radar pointed at the intersection. As you cross the intersection, each radar wave will take the same amount of time to reach him and your speed will be "0" mph, because you are not getting closer or farther away from him. The radar does not really measure your speed. It measures the closing speed of your car to the police unit. Is this getting confusing again?

Let me try to explain it this way; the only time

that radar is EXACTLY correct is if you are driving directly toward it or directly away from it. The more of an angle existing between the radar unit and the line you are traveling, the more inaccurate the radar becomes. Any error will always be in favor of the violator. It will measure a slightly lower speed, because it will be measuring the speed based on the closing distance between your vehicle and the radar, rather than your forward motion. The difference will not be very great but even one mile per hour may keep you from getting a ticket. You can increase the angle by staying in the driving lane, rather than the passing lane because most radar units will be in the oncoming lane or in the median. The wider the median is, the better off you are.

By staying in the driving lane you have, in most cases, also reduced your chances of the police radar being able to pick you up. Because most violators are found in the passing lane, officers angle or point the radar antenna so it will pick up cars in that lane. If a car or truck is behind you in the passing lane and you are in the driving lane, chances are the radar will register the speed of that other vehicle, before it locks onto yours. This can give you more warning and a little more time to slow down. In addition, the scenario I just set up can seem to sometimes confuse the radar and it will not give a reading on either vehicle until you get much closer.

I grant you that sometimes an officer will find a spot off the right side of the road where he can hide and clock you but more often than not, you will ''get your picture taken'' from the median or the opposite direction. Each thing you do to reduce your odds of getting stopped, boosts your average chance of not getting caught. Expecting the enemy to attack from your left is a logical action. When a cop does set up on the right side, your CB radio can usually warn you with plenty of time to slow down.

So we now have you using the driving lane, with your headlights off during the day. We can now address your third error. In that you were just relaxing. Speeding while avoiding detection takes concentration and no small amount of effort on your part. I would liken it to taking flying lessons. In spite of instruments and air traffic controllers, pilots are taught to constantly scan for other aircraft. The successful speeder also maintains that high degree of concentration. This book can only tell you what to look for. It is up to you to put the lessons into action.

You don't speed to save time because it makes very little difference on a long trip and no difference on a short one. I believe most of you speed because you find that driving at the speed limit is boring. If that is the case, then get rid of the boredom by honing your powers of observation to the best you can do. If you can get caught relaxing, then you can also get caught speeding!

Other than the obvious police car, what should you be looking for? For starters, always know the composition and topography of the median. If it is logical to expect the cop's sneak attack will come from that area, shouldn't you pay attention to it? The median (mall) can tell you much more than just how many littering slobs use that road. Get used to paying attention to the number of ruts or markings in the grass, made by turning cop cars. This will tell you where traffic enforcement is heaviest. Cops are creatures of habit and tend to look for speeders in areas where they have been successful in the past. An area with no mall marks can almost be considered a demilitarized zone. If the median is all chewed up, more caution is advised.

Often the median can't be crossed for quite some time. This is valuable knowledge for the average driver, yet do you know where these areas are on the interstates you routinely travel? A few miles of guide rail or culvert is almost a license to speed yet thousands of cars go by with their drivers unmindful of the bonanza. Sometimes I think the engineers working for highway departments hate cops and put up these barricades just to spite them. It is quite simple to use these areas to your advantage.

As you pass the last point where the officer can turn around, you simply slowly increase your speed until you see the next U-turn. You then slow down until you have passed the U-turn point by about a half mile, before starting to increase your speed again. This will tend to work because the added distance acts as a discouragement to any oncoming cops using moving radar. The officer must weigh the speed you are going, against the distance he has to chase you, when making his decision as to whether he should bother with you. Because of their intimate knowledge of the patrol area, many cops don't even bother to activate their radar in these difficult areas.

Many portions of the interstate system have guiderails on both sides of the road, in a manner that does not leave room for police cars to stop you. A classic example of this would be large bridges and tunnels. In these areas, cops are predisposed to ignore the speeder. The only option they have is to follow you until the road condition changes and Officer Neckvein is not noted for his great deal of patience. Easier victims exist and will be chosen.

On the other hand, special caution should be used when passing service areas, rest areas, and entrance ramps. By repeatedly leaving and entering the road, the officer is able to reduce the effectiveness of CB radios. Always watch for cars that suddenly appear behind you. If you did not notice them approaching, chances are it could be a cop who just pulled in behind you.

I realize, not all of you will have radar detectors or CB radios. In addition, even those of you who do have those items it would be foolish to depend on them exclusively. We have all heard the sermons about "defensive driving." Here's a few tips about defensive driving, interstate speeder style. They may also reduce your chances of having an accident but are mentioned here because they will often help you to avoid getting stopped.

How do you see a cop before he sees you? Even better, how do you "see" a cop before he comes into view? It's really quite simple. You establish an early warning system, letting others do the looking for you. There is only one way to do this. You must pay strict attention to the actions of the other highway users and instantly react to their actions. To do this, most of you must change the way you look at other traffic.

There is a term, used in accident investigations, called over-driving the headlights. It refers to a vehicle traveling at such a speed that it would be impossible to stop within the area illuminated by the car's headlights. Accidents are often caused by people who do not realize how long it will take to stop their vehicle. Speeding cops and race car drivers soon learn they must look for possible danger to the limit of their vision. By that, I mean they pay attention to the road, as far as they can see. It's important that you learn to do the same thing, not because you will be traveling as fast as a speeding cop, but because, by watching the traffic, two miles ahead of you, there will be some obvious clues as to where the cops are.

For instance, there is little reason for a person to hit the brakes, even for a split second, while traveling on a divided highway. Yet the natural reaction of many drivers when they see a cop car, is to do just that. If you see the brake lights flash, for even a split second, on any car traveling far ahead of you, your reaction should be to quickly slow down until you pass the point where the other car had braked. Always be on watch for those brake lights in the distance! Don't wait until you get to where the other car was, before slowing down. Do so immediately. Many times the other driver will have spotted a police car approaching. You and that cop will be closing on each other at a combined speed of about 125 to 150 mph. He will be within radar range in a matter of seconds. Don't wait until you see him. Anytime a car, far out in front of you, illuminates the brake lights, for even a split second, you should slow down until you are traveling at, or near the speed limit.

Pay attention to the oncoming traffic. You might be approaching a hill crest, the bottom of a hill, end of a straight stretch, a curve or other good ambush point. Is there a police car ahead, waiting to trap you? It's often possible to determine if a cop is there, by observing the actions of the drivers who are traveling (toward you) in the opposite direction. They have just driven by the ambush point and know if a cop is waiting for you. In the past, what did you do when you saw a cop? The vast majority of drivers slow down and don't speed up until they have traveled at least a couple of miles. Many of them also pull into their right-hand lane, especially the big rigs. Conversely, speeding cars approaching you are an indication that you too can safely speed. The approaching cars don't have to be flashing their headlights to be a warning to other drivers who are paying attention.

The actions of the oncoming motorists will often be caused by a cop car who already has a victim pulled over. We have all come upon the scene of some poor soul who is "feeding the bear." Traffic slows to a crawl as everyone suddenly gets religion. Don't you make that same mistake. If the cop is out of the car, and the radar unit activates, he has no way of knowing which car set it off. If he is in the car, the radar is only a danger to you while the cop car is still in view. Most cops ignore other speeders until the ticket is completed.

Now let's teach you another ruse that you can place in your bag of tricks until needed. Do you remember that in Chapter One, I pointed out how often many off duty cops speed? Assume for a moment, that in spite of all your efforts to avoid detection, you are caught going well above the speed limit, by an officer approaching you. What to do? Most drivers spike their brakes, bringing further attention to themselves, as their front bumper dips down, while clouds of blue smoke roll from all four tires. They then stare straight ahead, apparently in the belief that if you ignore a cop, maybe he will go away.

What is the cop doing? If he has, in fact, caught you speeding, he will be looking you and your car over real good, while deciding whether to chase after you. He will be considering factors such as your speed, the distance to the next place where he can reverse direction, and the possibility that you are an off duty cop. He won't want to go to the trouble of chasing you if he can't expect to give you a ticket. I already taught you how to pull over like an off duty cop. Now it's time for you to act the same way in this circumstance.

An off duty cop would establish eye contact with the officer in the police car. He would then either nod, or very casually wave with his left hand. If you try this while driving a rental car, it is even more apt to work because rental vehicles often are similar to detective cars. Does the thought of waving at a cop who just caught you speeding, send shivers up your spine? If so, just establish eye contact and casually nod your head. If he's not looking at you, forget about him, as it is very doubtful he is after you.

While we are on the subject of establishing eye contact with a cop, many of you panic when a police car pulls up next to you in the passing lane. As you and the cop travel along at about 60 mph, you lock your head and eyes straight ahead while you chant to yourself, "Please go away. Please go away. Please go away." I know that's what you're doing because sometimes I recall seeing your lips move! Consider the following:

1. If the cop wants you, by the time he is next to you, he will have had you.
2. Not looking at him won't cause him to change his mind.
3. By pretending you don't see him, you give the impression you are not paying attention to your driving.
4. If he does want to get your attention, you are making him angry by ignoring him.

For heavens sake, look at the man! If he makes eye contact with you, just nod. If he signals for you to pull over, just nod your head in the affirmative and safely pull over. The harder you make it for him, the less chance you will have at avoiding the ticket.

The next item that should receive your attention is under bridges. They're a favorite spot for cops to lurk. On any hot summer day, you can always find snakes in shaded glens, fish in the weeds, flies on garbage, and cops under bridges. It's actually quite pleasant under there. As long as a comfortable spot to sit is found, the cop figures why not justify his existence by turning on the radar while dozing or reading the sports section? There is always a gentle breeze as the semis rush by, even if it carries the odor of burned diesel fuel. So always remember trolls and cops love to hide under bridges. You have all heard the comment, ''You can never find a cop when you need one.'' Well, the next time you need one, look under a bridge.

As you are tooling down the highway, sooner or later you are certain to pass one of those ominous signs such as ''WARNING—Speed checked by aircraft.'' In the past, chances are it had the desired affect as you fearfully scanned the skies while your expression would remind someone of an old movie with the obligatory close up of the WWII bomber crews, looking for Luftwaffe fighters. While you searched the heavens, your speed would drop to near the speed limit.

Sucker!!!! It must have at least entered your mind! You're again being lied to by your government and it's been working! Shades of Tricky Dick and Watergate! If they were really working an aircraft speed trap in that area, do you think they would tell you? Sure, occasionally the airplane or helicopter will go up so they can piously claim they are telling the truth; however, you can bet it will be clocking traffic nowhere near the sign. The next time you see one of these signs, feel free to thumb your nose at it and give it the old Bronx cheer.

So where are all those damn airplanes and how can you possibly avoid them? The truth is they can usually be found sitting on the ground. The prohibitive expense of keeping them in the air eventually sinks through the skulls of even mindless bureaucratic police brass and politicians. When federal subsidies dry up, so does the aviation fuel.

Catching speeders from the air gives the cops a certain psychological benefit but with a little effort, you can neutralize the threat. The way I see it, to neutralize the threat from above, you have three choices. You can hire the military to come up with a ''stealth'' car cover that won't work but will cost billions. You can invest in a portable surface to air missile, that would stop this foolishness once and for all or you can simply find out where the speed traps are and slow down while going through them. On a hunch I suspect most of you will choose option three.

The aircraft needs ground support to write the tickets, and because catching speeders from the air is like shooting ducks in a barrel; more than one chase car is usually assigned. Clue #1, your CB radio will be reporting police cars situated with or near each other. The smokey reports will keep coming in at the same locations with lots of cars being pulled over in the same general area.

The cops in the airplane need points, between which the violators can be clocked. There is usually at least five of them in a row and they are always separated by the same distance, such as 2/10 of a mile. Clue #2, this requires the painting of spots or lines on the edges of the road. I mentioned them in the Chapter on RADAR. Contrary to popular belief, the cops in the sky can't grab you just anywhere. They need those markers. As a result, the airplanes always work the same stretch of road, when they do work. Always be on the lookout for those white lines painted on the shoulder of the road. Often they are painted on both sides of the interstate so the pilot need only fly in a large circle while the observer clocks speeders in both directions. The white squares or lines usually touch the fog lines on each side of the road but are not painted across the traveled part of the lane. They do not resemble race finish lines or crosswalks because of the chance some driver might get confused. Look for them on the shoulders and between the lanes.

Once you have them located simply slow down. Even if you are in the process of being clocked, this speed catching technique can only determine your average speed between two of the points. If you think there is a chance you are in the process of becoming a victim, by just slowing down you will be reducing your average speed and will no longer end up as a keeper. After traveling a couple of miles, resume your speed. Remember, you only need to slow down enough so your average speed is below the tolerance and can speed back up when you pass the last mark.

If you travel the same stretch of road often, you now should be able to locate exactly where the aircraft will work and you will know to slow down when going through there. Keep in mind that if poor flying conditions exist, such as haze or a low ceiling, then there will be no games played with the airplane. You can just disregard having to slow down in the trap area. The flight will also be cancelled if high winds exist or if the condition of the shoulder limits visibility. In northern states, the shoulder might be covered with snow or the marks may be impossible to see due to the road salt making the whole shoulder look white.

These airplane capers are considered a special detail and are most often done during the day shift. The truth is I have never heard of one in operation after 4 P.M. but that doesn't mean some police agency won't try it. I can't imagine even a sheriff's department would be crazy enough to try running one at night.

I have repeatedly mentioned the use of the CB radio. The proper title is "Citizens Band" radio and, like radar detectors, no speeder should be without one. They should be installed by a professional with the antenna "tuned" so you will be certain to get the maximum range from them. Like the radar detector, if you use it improperly, the result could spell disaster.

The value of a CB radio comes, not from speaking but from listening. When set at channel 19 you will have an early warning system that will give you a constantly updated location of virtually all the marked police cars in the area and for most of the unmarked cars too. You will know where radar has been set up and where the patrols are limited. You will know where a patrol has someone pulled over and where any accidents are. It is not necessary to ask, other drivers volunteer the information. Keep in mind this is just one more tool and not the answer to avoiding any and all tickets.

Regrettably, when a CB radio is first installed, I believe it gives off some kind of invisible ray that tends to make the proud new owner act like an ass. If you can overcome the effects of this syndrome, then you will find this tool fun to use and lifesaver. All too often new owners just can't resist becoming a "ratchet jaw." They also tend to forget that those radio waves are being monitored by many people. Unlike your telephone, the cop does not need a warrant to eavesdrop on your radio conversations. Want to irritate a cop in a big way? Drive down the road behind him while giving "smokey reports" every two or three minutes. It won't take him long to figure who you are and it will take even less time to decide how to make your life miserable. Unless someone is calling for someone else to respond, keep your mouth shut. If you are asking for a "smokey report" more than once every thirty minutes, you are screwing up. Learn to listen.

Sooner or later you will find yourself using the radio to chat with another driver. Chances are he or she will be a trucker or someone who frequently travels the same route as part of their business. Don't be bashful, ask if they know anyone who was recently stopped and at what speed they were stopped. It is an excellent way to help you in determining what the tolerance in any area is.

There is almost a foolproof way of finding out what the tolerance is but it takes some work. Ask a judge. Even better, ask a bunch of judges. That's not as crazy as it may sound and it really is almost foolproof. If you travel the same stretch of road frequently, it would be well worth the effort. Here's how you do it.

Compose a letter and send it to the judges who

have jurisdiction in the area you travel. You tell them you are doing a "study" or "report" and would appreciate their help. If they make the mistake of thinking this is some kind of academic venture, that isn't your fault. You are doing a study, and you are making a report to yourself.

In the letter you ask him to complete the "attached survey form" and you assure him you do not need exact figures. Of course you include a self-addressed stamped envelope. The "form" should not be more than three typed pages with blanks to fill in or multiple choice answers to the questions. Make it as easy to complete as possible. Ask lots of dumb questions having to do with traffic court but include questions like:

During the last 90 days, of the speeding tickets your court has handled, how many were for speeding less than 5 mph over the speed limit?

How many were for more than 5 but less than 8 mph over the speed limit?

How many were for more than 7 but less than 10 mph over the speed limit?

How many were for more than 9 but less than 15 mph over the speed limit?

You get the idea but just in case you don't, a sample cover letter and survey is in the appendix. Am I a nice guy or what!?

Before I bring this chapter to a close, I have repeatedly promised to give you information on the best use of radar detectors, CB radios and how to drive differently so as to avoid getting caught. The fact is, what you have read has already taught you all you need to know about the CB and most of what you need to know about the radar detector and driving. In the interest of giving you your money's worth, I will again touch on these items; however, if you have been paying attention to what you have already read, this will be a review for you.

The radar detector performs only one function. For all the advertising dollars spent on touting their amazing capabilities, all they do is detect electromagnetic radiation. In laymans' terms, the thing goes beep when it receives certain types of radio waves. One of the things that puts out these waves is the police radar unit. Make no mistake about it, there are other sources of these waves that will set off most, if not all, radar detectors. All you need to know is that when the foolish thing goes beep, make sure someone else is going faster than you are! Slow down, but don't lock up your brakes, and maintain that slower speed for the maximum distance that your detector is capable of picking up radar waves.

Do not disregard a short beep! As you now know, many radar units are equipped with instant on/off buttons. If your unit goes off yet it indicates the source is quite far off, slow down anyway. Try to remember, at interstate speeds, the closing speed between your car and the cop may be as fast as 175 mph and that can cover a big chunk of real estate in a short time. In addition, the short warning may have been the officer using the instant on/off button to check the speed of someone traveling a mile or two in front of you.

If a tone indicates you may have just had your picture taken, take your foot off the gas but stay off the brakes. You of course realize, that if you have cruise control, then this won't slow you down. In that case, just turn off your cruise control and keep your foot off the gas! Depending on traffic and other variables, the radar unit sometimes fails to give a read out. Stay in the driving (right) lane as much as possible. If you are in the passing lane and your detector goes off, get into the driving lane as quick as you can and stay there. It is distinctly possible the radar will lock onto someone else.

Always try to use another vehicle in front of you as a shield. Trucks work best. When using this shield, don't get careless and be sure to watch the traffic behind you. If someone is closing on you quickly, let him pass and use him as a new shield. Don't forget, in some jurisdictions, such as the Province of Ontario, Canada, the "fuzzbuster" is illegal.

The CB radio should always be monitored on channel 19 but rarely used for transmitting. Remember that many officers also have the radios and you should be cautious when you do choose to transmit. One of the biggest dangers when using a CB radio is that you will become complacent. They will help you keep tabs on almost all the police cars in view, being especially useful in reporting the old reliable radar speed trap, yet don't forget, the cops also know this and do their best to surprise you.

Pay attention to the other traffic. The drivers who are far ahead of you and the drivers approaching you, will often warn you when danger is near and help you to determine when danger is not near.

Keep your headlights off during the day time as

that is a signal that brings you to the attention of the traffic cop. Use them to flash at people so as to get them to move but avoid tailgating.

There is one more important detail to remember!!! Don't leave a copy of this book where the officer will see it.

Have a safe trip!

CHAPTER 10

The Generic Unmarked Car

This book would hardly be considered comprehensive without covering the ever dangerous specter of the unmarked car. Some cops dislike them while others love them. Speeders should despise them. Depending on your feelings toward cops in general, you may be pleased or just interested to know that driving an unmarked car is much more dangerous than patrolling in a typical marked unit. Other drivers often fail to perceive the unmarked car as an emergency vehicle and consequently do not react to them as the officer would anticipate. This can make for some exciting fun and games at times. Oh, the thrill of responding to an emergency through heavy traffic, while everyone seems to be doing their best to scare the hell out of you! The only real enjoyment I got while driving one, was watching people's faces as they suddenly realized they were passing a cop car. Let's see what we can do to keep you from finding yourself in the same situation.

When I advocated you remain in the right lane as much as possible, it was for numerous reasons. In addition to keeping more distance between an approaching radar unit and your car, by staying in the driving lane, you get other rewards. It's also obvious that when you stay in the right lane you will also increase the number of "radar shields" in front of you. As mentioned before, other traffic will sometimes cause the radar to miss you or take longer to lock onto you.

You will also find that, because you are in the driving lane and need to check traffic behind you before passing, you will be looking behind you more often. Consequently, you will have a more frequent picture of the traffic in that area. To put it bluntly, most interstate travelers have their heads up their butts and pay far too little attention to the traffic behind them. When an officer in an unmarked police car tries to sneak up on them, he is usually successful at completing a pace before ever being noticed by the violator. You made it easy for him!

If you learn to constantly monitor the traffic behind you, then you have again decreased your chances of getting caught. I can picture many of the readers saying to themselves, "I already do that." I hate to burst your bubble but no you don't! Want to test yourself? Have a passenger in the car occasionally ask you to tell about the cars behind you. Unless you glance up to check your mirror, as often as not, you won't be able to even get the number of cars correct. If you frequently check the rear- and side-view mirrors, then you will never become one of the half asleep idiots who manage to pull into the passing lane in front of a police car, or sit in that lane while the cop is trying to get by. You don't want to bring yourself to the attention of the cop at all. To do so while aggravating him at the same time can be very costly.

At night, you should know every set of headlights behind you and you should also be aware as to what vehicle they belong. If there is suddenly a set of lights you can't explain, then beware. Unless they're attached to the cab of a truck, assume they're attached to a cop car. Unless you just passed an entrance ramp, the only new lights to appear behind you will come from another speeder traveling faster than you or a cop, doing the same thing.

Either way, stay to the right, let the car pass, while you get a good look at it, and then just react accordingly. By that, of course I mean you can use the new speeder as your shield, if you are quite sure he is not a cop in an unmarked car. If he is a cop then you will know to behave when necessary. Try to remember, just as the radar operator is apt to stage his attack from the opposite lanes, the un-marked car can be expected to sneak up on you from behind.

Most unmarked cars can be placed into one of four categories. The first and most frequent thorn in the speeder's side, is the uniformed cop's un-marked car. It's almost always a full size police car that just happens to be painted another color. They're also the easiest to spot. The next category would be the cars assigned to detectives and the third would be the cars driven by police brass. Both of those categories are tougher to spot but are also much less dangerous to the speeder. Unless you are driving like a maniac, or do something to anger them, they tend to ignore the speeder as they believe they are much too important to waste precious time with a simple speeder. To activate their police radio and call for a patrol car, is most often, in their view, beneath their exalted position and dignity. Remember the police ego? Promotions multiply the effect. The higher the rank, the more they become legends in their own minds.

In truth, many of them travel at such a high rate of speed that they wouldn't notice a car going less than twenty miles over the speed limit, unless it was getting in their way. Once you learn to identify these cars, judge for yourself. You will often find them going in three digit figures. Stay out of the passing lane and they won't even notice you are speeding too.

If they are not going to bother you, why should we spend time teaching you how to recognize them? I have a number of very good reasons. The police ego comes into play if you are tailgating them, speed past them, or in some other way manage to create a little aggravation. You might think of them as the ''hibernating bears.'' Leave them alone and they won't even know you are near but poke a stick in their eye and life becomes exciting to the extreme! So who needs all that much excitement? They would tend to take such things as tailgating or road hogging, personally. If you have become a personal irritant, then one might call for a patrol officer to ticket you. I want you to be able to spot them so you can be certain to leave them alone, for your own sake.

Also, let's assume a car passes you at a high rate of speed and you also accelerate with the intention of using him as a shield. If it is a detective or cop type boss, he will be recognized as such by the approaching patrol and the cop will ignore him, catching you. If you have also recognized the detective as a cop, you will have enough sense to not use him as a shield.

The fourth type of unmarked car is the one you will have the most trouble identifying and they do present a big problem to speeders. For want of a better description, let's call them the "funny cars." They are uniform police officer's patrol cars but are of the more exotic, expensive breeds. Fortunately for the motoring public, the cost of these cars causes their numbers to be limited. Some examples of cars that have been used, are the Ford Mustang, Chevy Camaro and Pontiac Trans Am. They are often paid for, at least in part, by our bungling bureaucrats in Washington, the same ones that give away airplanes.

Each of the four types of unmarked cars have unique characteristics and many "clues" in common. Regrettably there will often be times when nothing will offer a foolproof means for you to positively identify a car as an unmarked police unit. You will just have to use your good judgement. Try to get into the habit of checking each car you see. Many a speeder has passed an officer who has then paced them, resulting in an issued ticket.

Before we go any further, please again note this chapter's title. I did not use the term "generic" just because I thought it would be cute. I can tell you what is generally the norm, yet there will always be exceptions and you must keep this in mind while on the road. What I will be pointing out will be the USUAL case but each police agency in this big country is an independent entity and each of these "rules" will be bent or broken somewhere. I'm sure some police outfit, somewhere out there, is using a cattle truck or Volkswagen van as an unmarked car but that is not the norm. I try to give you what is valid most of the time but unless we get one federal police force, differences will exist as you travel from one jurisdiction to another.

With these points in mind, let's address the subject of the first and most common variety of unmarked car. These vehicles perform the same function as their marked counterparts. Sometimes they may be used in a parked position while the occupant is running radar and calling out the intended victims to other officers. Most often they are just used on patrol in lieu of a marked unit. Let's put one under the microscope and see what looks different from the other highway users.

For starters, consider the make, model and body style. Whenever you see a marked cop car, note what make and model that vehicle is. As this book is written, there are three vehicle models making up the vast majority of cop cars. The vehicles most frequently used are the Dodge Diplomat, the Chevrolet Caprice, and the Ford Crown Victoria. The unmarked cars will usually be the same make and models being used for marked police cars in the same organization.

If you were responsible for maintaining a fleet of vehicles, wouldn't you buy all of the same kind so as to save money when stocking tires and other repair parts? Police agencies also sometimes purchase cars in a joint bid for that year. The bids for police cars are also going to include the bids for the unmarked units, so they are often identical, except for the paint jobs.

Don't forget different car companies may win in subsequent years so you may find different makes of cars in the same fleet. For example, it is possible the same agency may have 1989 Fords, 1990 Chevrolets, and 1991 Dodges. Learn to make a mental note of the headlight/grill configurations you see on police cars. It has long been the practice of the military to memorize enemy ships and aircraft by their silhouettes. It wouldn't hurt you to learn what the popular cop car silhouettes are and watch for them in your mirrors.

It might help for you to know that the cars purchased for police also are available to the general public. For example, if you went into a Ford dealership and told the friendly salesman you wanted the cheapest Crown Victoria he could order for you, the results would look like an unmarked car, unless you, like everyone else, surrendered to the seemingly unlimited list of available accessories. The same is, of course true for the other car companies. Regardless of the make of the vehicle, the police car looks exactly like what it is; a full size, stripped down, cheap as possible, luxury car with as little of the luxury as possible left intact.

During the 1980s, passenger cars began to shrink, yet police needed to keep their cruisers full size. Eventually the only cars big enough to fulfill the need, were those considered American made "luxury" cars. The people responsible for purchasing police cars took a dim view of surrounding the officers in leather seats and plush interiors, at their expense and made their objections known to the auto makers. The car companies, not being stupid, responded to the need. As a result, you can expect cop cars to look like economy versions of the same models sold to the public.

With this in mind, how is the exterior of the car affected? Expect no glitz. They should be all one color with no vinyl roofs or fancy trim. The hub caps are usually the cheapest that can be bought and the tires won't be anything that would tend to "dress up" the car. You might find an occasional pin stripe or chrome trim on the sides but economy will be the operative word. If it costs extra, it won't be there. Any trim found on these cars is there because the companies insist on putting it on, not because the police purchasing agents asked for it. Don't expect to find landau roofs, two-tone paint jobs, "special edition" designations, etc.

Look for a spotlight mounted on the post, in front of the driver's door. Remember, because the cars are often purchased as a package deal, it is not uncommon for the unmarked units to be delivered with the exact same equipment as the marked ones, including the spotlight. The front seats will also be designed for economy and utility. Don't expect to see the tops of bucket seats. The "sixty/forty" seat is most common. That's a bench type seat that's split so about sixty percent is allocated for the driver and forty percent for the passenger.

These days you can't buy a new or used car without becoming a mobile advertisement for the car dealer. It may be a decal on the rear bumper, a frame surrounding your license plate, or both. One thing is certain. Some place on the back of the car will be something that will prominently tell all who look, exactly where the car was purchased. Unless you firmly insist to the contrary, it will be slapped on the rear of your nice new automobile before it leaves the car lot. Police cars are generally purchased in large lots and "prepped" by employees of the police agency rather than at a car dealership. Considerable special effort and expertise is required to install flashing headlights, emergency light bars, PA systems, multiple channel radios and other gadgets that make a cop's car his office. Why tell you this? If you take the time to look and you notice a fairly new car does not have a dealer's logo or advertisement mounted in plain view on the rear, it's a good bet you have found an unmarked cop car of some type. Even if the police cars are "prepped" by a car company dealer, chances are the police agency will forbid the placing of advertising on their cars.

About the only other cars that consistently don't display dealer logos are rental cars. Most of those companies now use the same gimmick to advertise for themselves. Get into the habit of looking for the car dealer stickers on cars you overtake or that pass you. If one is visible or is from a dealer in an area far from where you are, then the chances are the car is not being driven by a cop and you need not concern yourself with it.

Another point to look for when deciding if a car is a cop's, would be the vehicle's body type. I have never seen a full size, two door car used for police work. Cops need to have four doors so prisoners can be easily transported and so people may be placed in the back seat for interviews at accidents or crime scenes. Even some of the police "funny cars" that I have seen, were of the four door variety. Would your average Police Chief or Commissioner settle for a two door car? I think not!

Another clue that might also help you spot an unmarked car is to look at the back side of the front seat. Some units have cages mounted between the two seats for the officer's safety. Many unmarked cars have these cages attached to the rear of the front seat, but they may fold down when not in use. You might be able to spot mounting brackets, or the cage itself, mounted between the front and rear doors, if you pay attention. These cages are often in plain view for anyone who looks for them and are an instant tip off you are looking at a cop car.

Look for a tow hitch. Very few police cars need or have them, so the existence of one indicates the car is not a cop. Many of the large "cop type" cars purchased by civilians are bought for towing purposes. When a police agency does have something to tow, such as a boat, they generally will choose to mount the hitch on a marked police unit. While you are looking for a bumper hitch, check out the license plate. Again, the lack of creativity by the police is nothing short of mind-boggling.

You will often see unmarked cars with license plates that say "POLICE." It will help if you have already taken the time to check out what kind of plates are mounted on the marked police cars. They often are similar. As an example, the New York State Police presently have small initials "DSP" on all the police car registrations used by uniform patrols. It stands for "Division of State Police." The normal size plate numbers will then have one letter indicating to what troop the car is assigned. Many other police departments have registrations with the word "OFFICIAL" written under the numbers. If you get into the habit of looking at police car registration plates, it won't take long for you to figure out any similar codes in your particular area.

When we looked at your car with the intention of making it less prone to getting a ticket, we mentioned bumper stickers at length. Again the subject comes up. Unmarked cars are not likely to have bumper stickers unless they are of the "School's Out—Drive Carefully" variety. It is also obvious the back window will not be decorated with the college name and emblem of the officer's alma mater.

Most decals will be conspicuous by their absence. Would you expect a police car to need a parking or landfill permit displayed on the window? Would the Police Commissioner not be a little bit miffed if he were to see one of his cruisers bearing the proud declaration "This car climbed Mount Baldy" or some other equally inane tourist prattle! Conversely, the existence of decals and bumper stickers indicate the car is NOT a police vehicle.

If you are still uncertain about a particular vehicle, I suggest you count the number and type of antennas. Also note where they are mounted. Simply put, unmarked police cars will need to have antennas. They may also have a regular AM/FM type radio antenna. They might have a CB antenna but it is doubtful the car would be equipped with a cellular telephone antenna. In the future, as prices go down, and the natural resistance to change begins to erode, police cars will all be sporting cellular telephone antennas as they are an invaluable cop tool. For now, the presence of a cellular telephone antenna would indicate the car is not one driven by a ticket writing policeman. Again, what do you see on the marked police units in your area? That is what you can expect the unmarked units to be sporting. Also remember, a cellular telephone might be an indication of one of the ''Police Brass.''

The above information will do you no good unless you can identify the different types of antennas. We can start with the regular car radio antenna, usually located on the passenger side front fender. Let's see how good your eyesight is. Look at the top of the antenna. Notice a small round ball at the tip? If you suspect a car is a cop and there is no small ball at the top of his car antenna, your suspicions are justified. In addition, as you look at the length of the antenna, AM/FM car radio antenna telescope and you should see the points where one portion slides into the other, to raise or lower it. The small round ball at the tip, is part of that assembly. Police antennas, on the other hand, MUST remain the correct length to transmit properly and there is no noticeable change in the thickness. They are all one piece. I grant you, this may be tough to spot but if a "suspect" car is passing you at a speed slightly faster than you are going, you can get a pretty good look. Don't judge a car as NOT being a police car just because his antenna is normal. His police antenna may be elsewhere. Most police cars now come with a good AM or AM/FM radio because the car companies build them that way.

Look for police band antennas mounted most often on the roof or the center of the trunk lid. Don't be surprised if the cop car is sporting both. It may be radio equipped so as to be able to talk to a number of different agencies. The big whip antennas of the 1950s and 1960s are no longer prevalent and now are most often used by ham radio operators. Expect the modern police antenna to be a thin stiff piece of wire, from four to twenty inches long. It might also be a larger unit that looks very similar to a CB radio antenna. If this is the case, look to the base. CB radios are almost always installed in passenger cars with the black coaxial cable leading from the base, to the nearest window. Police radios can be expected to be more permanently installed. The cable leading from the antenna will not normally be visible.

The cellular telephone antennas are very distinctive. They are almost always mounted at the center top of the rear window and begin by coiling upward for about two inches, like a small spring, before they straighten. They are usually colored black and are about 15 to 24 inches long.

For those of you who are not familiar with Citizen Band radios, I guess it will also be necessary to describe the antennas used with them. They come in various styles, some short and some long. Expect them to be mounted by a magnet or clamped to the rain gutter, with the thick black cord leading from the base to the nearest window. The base may be colored gray but so are some police antennas. You will see some of them that appear to have a wire coiled around the complete length of the antenna and they often have a portion, near the bottom, that is thicker and runs for about 2 ½ to 4 inches. Expect to see these antennas mounted along the edge of the trunk lid or attached to the rain gutters that run above the car's doors. Remember, almost all CB radios are installed after the car is purchased and they look that way. They may also be mounted in tandem with two identical antennas on opposite sides of the vehicle. If so, expect the two antennae to be identical. If the two antennae are different sizes, then it may be a cop.

I mentioned you might want to look at the inside of the "suspect vehicle" (how's that for a little reverse cop jargon?). When you do, look for a few more items. Remember how easy it is to see radar detectors in other people's cars? Unmarked police cars certainly don't need radar detectors so if you see one in a car, is it not logical to then assume that vehicle is not of the unmarked police car variety?

Look for a portable revolving light or a radar unit sitting at the center of the dashboard, or a radar console on the dash, in front of the steering wheel. Don't mistake them for a radar detector. Most radar detectors are now mounted on the visor with their curly tailed power cords in plain view, and are quite compact.

Check out the occupants. Is that a prisoner in the back seat? Wouldn't that give you a good reason to suspect a cop car!! All kidding aside, if you see a car that you suspect may be a cop and there is a guy in the back seat who seems to be leaning forward, while not having a good time, you have found a cop car. The prisoners will be very forlorn looking souls who, because of the handcuffs, seem to be constantly leaning forward in their seats. They also may be seen leaning way back with their pelvic area pushed upward. If they are handcuffed with their hands behind their back, this is the least uncomfortable position, especially if they are seat belted too, as is the custom.

If it is a detective's car transporting a prisoner, expect the cops in the front seat to be wearing dress clothing or business suits, while the ''bad guy'' in the back will be dressed differently. Once you know what to look for, detectives stand out like a sore thumb. Don't forget, if any cop is transporting a prisoner, it is highly unlikely he will stop you. Just leave him alone so he won't be tempted to call one of his uniformed brothers.

While we are on the subject of detectives' cars, there are a few more tricks you can use to help to identify them. Virtually all the hints given for the unmarked patrol cars are also valid with respect to the detectives' cars. Although some of the cars are also full size, most detectives drive four door medium size American cars, such as the Pontiac 6000 or Chevrolet Citation. Decals and car dealership advertisements will be missing. The antennas will be obvious to those who bother to look for them. Like the ones used by the uniformed officers, the police detectives' cars will all be cheap versions of those available to the public. Their cars are used, not for exciting chases but to get them from one interview to another.

With the few exceptions involving the deep undercover cops such as those working narcotics and having access to gobs of Federal money, the exotic cars you see detectives driving in the television shows, are nonexistent. The few undercover cops who do drive the ''deep cover'' cars should never consider taking the chance of blowing their cover to catch a speeder. Detective cars are used for the simple act of transportation and most could be outrun by a talented kid on a rusty, homemade skateboard.

Let's now totally explode the rest of the image television has created of America's super crime busters. The average detective is more apt to be a pot-bellied, gray haired, middle-aged, burned out road cop, who finally got promoted, rather than a fleet-footed, handsome stud in designer clothing. It is more likely his gun will be found in his car's trunk or under the front seat, covered with rust, than in a classy quick draw shoulder holster. Most of them look like bored traveling salesmen. They may wear a mustache but beards won't be permitted and hair will be conservatively cut. Expect to see them in dress shirts with ties loosened. Look for a sports jacket thrown over the front seat.

The "funny cars" mentioned at the beginning of this chapter will often be tough to spot but will not be impossible. Although often paid for, at least in part, by federal dollars, the concept that it will look like a stripped down economy version of the same model sold to the public, is still valid. Again, most of the points brought out earlier with respect to the full size police car will also be applicable. The driver will be in uniform, of course.

Last but not least, let us touch on the cars driven by the police hierarchy. They are also sometimes tough to spot, but not impossible. Be especially watchful for multiple antennae on American made luxury cars, driven by middle-aged males, who are ignoring the speed limit. The drivers will usually be alone and tend to be glaring constantly at the world in general. By the time they have battled their way up to one of the "ranking" positions, they don't generally seem to be very happy people. Again, most of the clues given for spotting the un-marked car will also apply to the cars driven by the police brass. There is one big exception. The cars are generally more plush yet not so plush as to annoy their political superiors. Look closely, they may also be dressed in uniform.

All this may seem like a lot to digest and many of the differences are small indeed, yet if you prac-tice by trying to judge each and every car that you pass, or that passes you, in no time at all you will be spotting the unmarked cars at a glance. Once you have perfected this capability, your chances of getting caught are reduced even further. In closing, don't forget the most important rule of them all:

PAY ATTENTION!

CHAPTER 11
For Truckers Only

How I wish there was a book the size of an encyclopedia I could write, just to help you guys, and ladies. I'm sure, as you read the previous chapters, at times your thoughts were "I know that already" or "that won't work if you're driving a truck." I'm certain you were also able to find many hints and helps, that you can use in the future. We both know the trucker is the highest taxed and least appreciated worker in our society and deserves any break he can get. I could go into a long dissertation about the trucker's difficult lifestyle but what would it accomplish? We also both know that companies, unions, governments, courts and cops have all found an easy victim, when looking in the driver's seat of an 18 wheeler.

Consider this; sometimes you have only yourselves to blame, especially when it comes to dealing with the cops. At least here I can give you some help. I can only help if you're willing to take some criticism, and then make an effort at correcting the existing problems. In addition to pointing out the circumstances that concern only truckers, I will also attempt to review the rest of the book with respect to what was mentioned earlier but applies to you, differently.

To begin, I may as well start by insulting you. I have tried very hard, to think of a way to cover this point without being insulting, but to no avail. Some of you guys are pretty big and I do value my life! Nevertheless, here goes . . . too many of you stink! I don't mean your driving, your sex life, your wages, your load, or your engine. I'm talking about good old-fashioned personal hygiene. Most of the long haulers who will be sitting in a cab while reading this, will be in desperate need of a shower or bath.

What's that got to do with getting a ticket? Are you thinking . . . "Good grief! Not another new Federal regulation!?" No, showers aren't required by law but if you think some cop will be inclined to let you go, after being forced to smell your last week's allotment of sweat, think again! Most cops don't like truckers to begin with. They look down on them as a social inferior. By not keeping yourself clean, you manage to reinforce that attitude. With the number of truck stops available, there is no excuse. I know this may seem preposterous but if you want the best possible chance to avoid a ticket, you better get clean and stay that way. There are enough truckers out there who don't smell bad, so we both know it can be done.

The majority of cops think of truckers in two distinct categories. There are the respectable "Company" drivers and then there are the "Independent" bums. This attitude came about because most of the big company drivers, following a set route, need not resort to driving unsafe vehicles, speeding, multiple log books, excessive driving hours, or even drugs to stay awake, so they can operate in the black. Because a larger share of independents break the law, all of them are more readily viewed as law breakers. Yes, I realize that since deregulation, many of the trucking companies are as bad or worse than many independents, but we are talking about the cop's perceptions, not reality.

Sure, now I have your dander up! If the paragraph about body odor didn't make you angry, then the one about independents might make your blood boil. Yes, that last paragraph is going to anger many an honest, hard working independent trucker, but for me to help you, you must realize the attitudes you are up against in order to fully appreciate why the forthcoming advice will be so useful. In addition, the same advice will help reinforce any already favorable opinions the cop may have when stopping the "company" man.

In addition to reducing fear and building the cop's ego, it is also important for you to convince him you are one of the "good guys," rather than "just another one of those damn law breaking trucker bums." More explanation is in order, isn't it?

Obviously, the cop will base his actions on the decisions he makes about you, during a very short period of time. The statue of the Lady of Justice, holding the scales, may be blindfolded but the cop's eyes will be wide open. Perhaps I could best explain my point by using an example.

The same cop pulls over two motorcycles, on the same day. Only one of them will get a ticket. One cycle is a "Harley" hog and the driver has long greasy, stringy hair hanging down his back. He is also in desperate need of a shave and is wearing a denim vest, proudly displaying his "colors." From his black garrison belt hangs a twelve-inch pig sticker, in a sheath. His bare arms are covered with tattoos.

The other motorcycle is a Honda touring unit, pulling a tiny trailer. That rider is wearing a helmet and protective clothing. Once stopped he opens his jacket to reveal a dress shirt and tie. His wife is riding on the back of the bike and greets the cop in a friendly manner. Based on the information you now have, would you agree the guy on the Harley Davidson got the ticket?

Now, lets add more information. When the Harley rider gives the cop his license, the picture on it shows a well-groomed and clean shaven man. The cycle is registered to a film company. The driver tells the cop, he is an actor, shooting on location and had permission to take the cycle on his lunch hour. He also says he stayed in makeup and costume as he went to the hospital to visit a young fan, who has cancer and the actor wanted to raise the young man's spirits.

On the other hand, the man on the Honda opened his wallet while looking for his license and managed to display a half dozen other tickets he had recently received. He also dropped paperwork, that the cop picked up. It was a receipt, indicating the man had recently been bailed after an arrest for trafficking in drugs. Now who got the ticket?

So what's my point? Simple. It doesn't matter if you are a child molesting mass murderer, a Chamber of Commerce "Citizen of the Year," or both. What matters is the impression you manage to give the cop. The better the impression, the better your chances of avoiding a speeding ticket. With that point in mind, is it so unreasonable for me to encourage you to keep clean?

We're going to do more than just get you cleaner. For starters, consider putting yourself into some kind of uniform. It gives you more of an appearance of legitimacy. A patch on the shoulder, indicating a safe driving award would be a nice touch, and a cheap investment. In addition to the obvious, this will also enable you to claim that getting a speeding ticket will ruin your chances for another safe driving award with a commensurate raise, at the end of this run.

If you can't bring yourself to give up the faded blue jeans with the holes in the knees or the lavender western shirt with matching belt buckle, I suggest you buy a few sets of coveralls, such as was the rage of bass fishermen a few years ago. They are easy to slide on or off and you can wear them over your other clothing. You can then leave them in your rig when you get out for other reasons. If that doesn't appeal to you, consider purchasing a few matching work shirts and slacks. Change them before they look slept in. While on the subject of changing clothing, always carry air tight plastic bags for your dirty clothing and put them in one of the storage units, rather than in your cab or sleeper. A trucker who smells of body odor, always has a truck that smells like a locker room.

Now that we're on the subject of the truck cab, let's take a tour of your humble little mobile domicile and see what changes we might make. Begin with the assumption that you have absolutely no right to privacy. By and large, there is almost always a way for a cop to LEGALLY get into your truck, even if you insist you don't want him in there! I'm not telling you what's morally right or wrong. I'm telling you what a cop can legally get away with, as a result of laws and court decisions. Just keep in mind, the right to the privacy you enjoy in your home, doesn't extend to the cab of your truck. Go with the assumption the cop will be entering your vehicle. By the time we are done, you will want him in there.

Before leaving on a run, take a half hour and clean the darn thing. I'm talking about everywhere, including under the seats, the dashboard, and side panels. The first time, you may have quite a job but after that, it will be easier. Look at the mattress in the sleeper. Do the stains look like it's been used in about a dozen too many X-rated movies? Pick up a couple of mattress covers and change them each trip. It wouldn't hurt to remove the entire mattress occasionally and air it out. Do I sound a little far-fetched? I'm not kidding at all! These are the things a cop uses to help him judge what kind of person you are.

Would the average wife be pleased if her husband showed all his friends their new bedroom set, when the bed wasn't made? Most truckers don't care or don't anticipate anyone will be looking in their "bedroom," so the sleeper area is almost always a mess. In my 20 years of police work, I have seen exactly one sleeper berth that was made up. Want to impress the cop you are a regular little boy scout who doesn't deserve a ticket? Make your damn bed! A slob is easier to ticket than a "good guy" and with the limited time a cop has to make a decision, these little things take on more importance. Please believe that isn't a pet peeve of mine but a valid point. Now that I'm retired, chances are I will never again enter a truck sleeper so it doesn't matter to me.

Let's redecorate your cab. You should have a few photographs in plain view. You may be the consummate family man or the hottest stud in the eastern corridor but your cab should contain photographs of "the loving family." Yes, I'm saying if you are single, get pictures of your brother's or sister's family. Any family will do, as long as the pictures make you appear to be a hard working family bread winner. Know any kids in wheelchairs or leg braces? What cop could give a "daddy" a ticket after seeing a picture like that? Be sure the little urchin scrawls some syrupy sweet mush like, "To daddy, I love you and come home soon, your little Johnny." An old father's day card signed by the wife, containing a prayer for your safe return, is also a nice touch. Be sure to have displayed, at least one scribbled picture from little Johnny. Any real family man with kids under age ten, will be glad to give you a few. You will find them hanging on their refrigerator door.

Do you know any young man or woman who recently became a cop? A picture of an officer in uniform, with a note on it indicating they ''never could have made it'' without your financial help, will also cause the average cop to pause and reconsider. One trucker told me the story about his friend who went to the trouble of having a bogus story printed up on newspaper stock. It told about how the man saved a cop from a burning police cruiser. The way the story was told to me, the man had two different copies. One indicated the incident happened a few years earlier on the east coast, and one on the west coast. The man would use the east coast copy while driving in the west and the west coast copy when he was in the east. The clippings were yellowed with age and looked authentic. Placed in the cab, where the cop would be sure to see it, almost guaranteed the man would get off with only a warning. He should have kept his mouth shut about it though. He bragged to his friends. One of them was offended by the whole idea and subsequently told every cop who would listen. That's how the trucker's great idea just ended up in print! I guess the moral of that story is: If you discover something that works great, you better keep it to yourself!

With all those props set up for the cop to see, you should leave the door wide open, giving the impression you have nothing to hide. By now you get the idea. Expect to get your cab searched. After all the work we went through redecorating your cab, you should want the cop to look inside. If he asks to look inside, smile and tell him, ''Sure Officer, if it will help you decide not to give me the ticket.''

Just as the four wheelers were warned, get rid of the empty beer and liquor bottles. Keep your pornography in one of the storage units. If you put it in your suitcase and then leave the suitcase in the sleeper, or if you slide magazines under your mattress, the cop will find it while he is snooping. You don't want to blow your image with porno magazines, do you? If you must carry a stash of the evil weed, or a few pills (for medicinal purposes only), all I will tell you is a lot more trucks get searched, than truckers.

There is more you can do, before leaving home, to help promote the best possible image to the cop. Pull out your permit book and set up a separate page for each state. Neatly, put them in alphabetical order, with marked tabs. You want to appear to be a professional, don't you? Trying to find a particular tax receipt by going through two dozen tattered envelopes, while the cop is standing there waiting for you, is not in your best interest. Also, don't wait for the cop to ask for your permit book. Offer it to him when he first walks up to you. You should offer him your log book at the same time, even if it's incomplete. He will appreciate the honesty.

While we are on the subject of the log book, a properly completed, accurate book, tells the cop much about you. Need I elaborate? Again, neatness counts. Lest you forget, save your humorous lines for the diners. I am referring to such prize-winning comments as "I ain't hauling logs," in response to being asked for your log book. You may think it's cute and it makes a good story to tell other truckers but it's not the impression you want to make to avoid a ticket. Cops have a great sense of humor, but only if they are the ones telling the jokes.

With the onset of more and more rules regarding "HAZMAT," cops will be frequently asking for your shipping papers. Are they neat and in proper order or do you have copies of your last six trips and need to shuffle through them? Offering them, before being asked, will also be a big help to you. At other times, store them in the driver's door.

Don't be afraid to ask the cop to write up an equipment violation, instead of the speed. Impress upon him you were given an unreasonably small amount of time to complete your run, by your boss, and you were trying your best to get the job done while speeding no more than necessary. Every cop can relate to the concept of the demanding, inconsiderate boss. If he writes you the equipment ticket, the boss will have to pay, won't he?

Try telling him about a MINOR emergency at home that will gain his sympathy. You want to become a living, breathing human being, rather than just another number. The cop can relate to someone who has problems at home and is unable to leave work to fix them. He also understands the stress that's created and that sometimes people speed because they are upset.

Do you need a few examples to get the right idea?

I would try telling him, "I just telephoned home and found out my spouse forgot to open the garage door before leaving with the new car. She was on her way to the school to pick up our two children. It seems one of them was at track practice and caught a discus with his mouth and only last week the kid got new braces! The other child was waiting in the principal's office after setting a false fire alarm. My wife is in hysterics and is blaming me because I am never home. I was just trying to finish this run and get home, before something else happened."

Note, I said to tell the cop about MINOR emergencies. If you told him someone was critically injured, or something too outrageous, you might find yourself with a police escort. How would you explain your way out of that? He also might decide you are lying because he has heard nothing of the big disaster you've so vividly described. Keep it simple.

Sitting high up in a truck gives you an excellent view of the road but creates a dilemma when pulled over by a cop. Do you remain in the truck, requiring Officer Neckvein to look (or climb) up to you, or do you climb down from the cab? Let's get back to the basics this book stresses. How can you best reduce the cop's fear while building his ego?

Unlike a car, if you remain in the vehicle, you place the cop at a big disadvantage. With respect to his ego, he will have to be looking up at you. He will also be very concerned about his personal safety. He can't even see what's in your hands or who else is in the cab, until he has made like a monkey, up the side of your rig. When he does get to peer into your window, both his hands will be busy, just holding on. His only other option is to remain on the ground, trying to be heard over your idling rig and the passing traffic. He will still not be able to see your hands or any other possible dangers to him. If you get down, you will present a danger to him and yourself, from the traffic. He will also not know what danger lurks in your cab. You're damned if you do and damned if you don't! I guess the only solution is buy a glass bottom truck!

The truth is you can choose to stay or get down, if done with a little bit of common sense and a dose of sucking up to the cop. Either way, it's important your driver's side cab door will remain open by itself. Now is the time to make whatever alterations are necessary to accomplish this. If you choose to get down, then exit with all your paperwork. Walk to the front of your truck and turn so you are facing the driver's side headlight, about six to eight feet in front of the truck. The cop can see you as he is walking past the side of your rig. He will also see your hands are full of your permits. As he walks by your open driver's door, a glance up will assure his safety. Don't forget to leave the sleeper curtain wide open too.

He now has the option to walk past you before speaking, requiring you to turn to face him. He then will have both you and the front of your rig in his eyesight, and can also see the approaching traffic. You can casually pivot so your back is facing the grill of your truck, when he reaches you. Your actions put him in the same favorable position. You have successfully reduced his fear as much as you possibly could, before even starting to speak to him. If you take one step toward the shoulder of the road, you will both also be protected from the passing traffic, by your rig.

The only other good option is to open your door wide before he reaches you. Turn in your seat so he can get a good look at you and have your hands where he can see them. One hand on the door, and your other hand holding the permit book seems to work very well. As the cop approaches, preferably before he even speaks to you, ask him, "Would you like me to stay up here or would you prefer I get down?" In doing so, you have shown him that no immediate danger exists, that you are cooperative, and have placed Officer Egotist firmly in charge. Nice job!

Last but not least, let's cover the trucker's unofficial title for the road cop, "SMOKEY." It's often shortened to a sort of nickname by dropping the "Y" and just calling him "SMOKE." Should you use it or not? As mentioned in an earlier chapter, speaking to any cop by his rank or by his official title (trooper, deputy, officer, etc.) is best, but I don't know of any cop who was offended by being called "SMOKEY," so if it helps you speak to him in a more friendly manner, go for it. A last word of caution would be, watch the cop's facial expression the first time you call him Smokey and if he grimaces or looks displeased, don't do it again!

CHAPTER 12

If The Cop Reads The Book, Too

While I was in the process of writing this book, the one point voiced by the few people who were given a preview was; "What if I'm doing exactly what the book recommends and the police officer smiles at me while he says, 'I read the book too'?" The answer is simple. You will find yourself in the same situation you would have been in if you had never read the book and you may be getting the ticket. You also stand an excellent chance of still avoiding it.

Most of the recommendations that were covered in this book, have repeatedly been successfully used on the side of the road. With the exception of Sister Mary Sweetness, who may have to find a new charade, it's doubtful any cop will change his basic program, after reading this book. By that, I mean the cop may check out the validity of clergy a little farther but he will still let them go, if that's his program.

Many officers don't even realize what motivates them to let one person go and ticket another. If this book causes them to be more aware of their motivation, it should also make them appreciate, even more, the occasional person who makes an effort at reducing his fear while playing up to his ego.

As in every other walk of life, each police officer is a different human being, with different responses to stimuli and different attitudes. Sure, the existence of this book will anger some cops but most of the angry ones will never read it. Those that take the time to review it will soon realize the book only encourages people to act in the manner the cop would want them to act. Nothing has taken away his ability to decide when to pick up the pen and when to leave it idle.

Yes, I've let the cat out of the bag with respect to how radar works and the tricks you can use to try to avoid it. So what? If they work, you won't get caught and if they don't, why should the cop care, or even know if you possess that information?

So, if a cop ever says to you "I read the book too," your proper reply should be "What book?"

Appendix

Sample Letter To A Judge

April 1, 1991

John Q. Enforcelaw
Justice of the Peace
Town of Speedtrap
Ketchum County
191 Traffic Court Way
Speedtrap, U.S.A. 00000

Your Honor:

You, and a group of your colleagues have been selected as a result of the large number of cases adjudicated before you with respect to traffic violations on interstate highways. The solicited information will be used to help in formulating a thesis with respect to driving trends in the 1990s. Your answers will be grouped together with other courts' responses. At no time will you or your court be singled out or mentioned by name in the study.

It would be greatly appreciated if you would take a few minutes to fill out the attached questionnaire, consisting of only 20 questions, and then return it in the enclosed, self-addressed, stamped envelope. If this is inconvenient, would it be possible to have a secretary, bailiff, or court clerk complete the attached item? Exact figures are not necessary and your best estimate would be a great help. Thank you for your trouble.

Respectfully,

_____

Sample Questionnaire

Please complete the following 20 questions using an estimate. Exact figures are not required.

1) What portion of your court's time is spent with cases initiated as a result of traffic offenses?

   _____ 10% or less
   _____ more than 10% but less than 25%
   _____ more than 24% but less than 50%
   _____ more than 49% but less than 75%
   _____ more than 74% but less than 85%
   _____ more than 85%

2) Of the traffic arrests handled, how many are alcohol related? _____%

3) What % of the court's time is used to process alcohol related cases? _____%

4) Of the traffic arrests handled, how many are issued as a result of an accident?
_____%

5) What percent of the court's time is used to process cases involving accident related cases?
_____%

6) What percent of the cases presented to your court result in the defendant pleading guilty in the first instance? _____%

7) How many trials do you average per month?
_____(number of cases, NOT %)

8) Of the not guilty pleas, what percent never go to trial as a result of their pleading guilty to a reduced charge? _____%

9) What percent of your traffic cases are for speeding violations on interstate highways?
_____%

10) What percent of the tickets mentioned in question #9, alleged a speed of 100 MPH or more?
_____%

11) What percent alleged a speed between 90 and 99 MPH? _____%

12) What percent alleged a speed between 85 and 89 MPH? _____%

13) What percent alleged a speed between 80 and 84 MPH? _____%

14) What percent alleged a speed between 75 and 79 MPH? _____%

15) What percent alleged a speed between 71 and 74 MPH? _____%

16) What percent alleged a speed of 70 MPH? _____%

17) What percent alleged a speed of 68 or 69 MPH? _____%

18) What percent alleged a speed of 66 or 67 MPH? _____%

19) Where the speed limit is 55 MPH, what percent alleged a speed of 62 to 65 MPH? _____%

20) Where the speed limit is 55 MPH, what percent alleged a speed of 56 to 61 MPH? _____%

About The Author

JAMES M. EAGAN wrote his first speeding ticket nearly a quarter of a century ago, as a young air policeman, stationed in Alaska. After his military discharge, he was sworn in as a trooper in the New York State Police in June of 1970. His first experience with policing interstates came shortly after his academy graduation when he was assigned to patrol the Cross Westchester Expressway, one of the busiest roads in the nation.

During the next 20 years and nearly a million miles, he continued to advance in rank, eventually commanding a number of State Police stations in upstate NY. In 1988, he was again promoted and found himself supervising the day to day police operations for 1/4 of the 500 mile long New York State Thruway.

During his career he became recognized in courts as an expert on speed, was a certified Radar, Vascar, and Moving Radar operator, and supervised both State Police Radar teams and aircraft speed enforcement details.

Since retiring from police work he has devoted his time to the completion of this book. His efforts have yielded a comprehensive yet entertaining look at why speeding tickets get written. His candor is nothing short of amazing.